PAPERCRAFT
Colouring Book

Clare Beaton

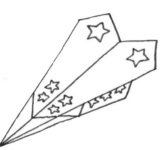

CONTENTS

b small publishing
www.bsmall.co.uk

How to use this book

Place the book on a flat surface and carefully cut out the page that you want to make. Colour in the ready-drawn shapes. Some shapes need to be coloured in on both sides. Use coloured pencils, crayons, felt-tips or paints. Use fairly thick paint and wash your brush between colours. Leave the pages flat to dry.

Some things you will need:

❖ coloured pencils, crayons, felt-tips or paints
❖ a pencil
❖ tracing paper
❖ sticky tape
❖ scissors
❖ paper or card

Templates

Here is a way to trace simply and successfully from a template.

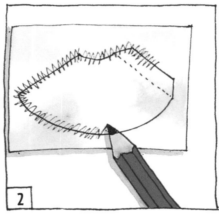

Tape a piece of tracing paper over the template. Trace one of the shapes with the pencil.

Turn over the tracing paper and scribble over the lines with the pencil.

Turn over again and tape on to some card or paper. Retrace firmly over the lines. Remove the tracing paper.

© b small publishing ltd., 2014

Original individual titles and copyright dates:
Cars and Trucks (2002), Farm Animals (2001), Paper Dinosaurs (2002), Paper Dolls (2000),
Paper Gifts (2002, 2010), Paper Planes (2000), Under the Sea (2002), Wild Animals (2001)

1 2 3 4 5

Design: Louise Millar Editorial: Sam Hutchinson Production: Madeleine Ehm

Printed in China by WKT Co. Ltd.

ISBN: 978-1-909767-43-0

British Library Cataloguing-in-Publication Data.
A catalogue record for this book is available from the British Library.

SILVER ARROW SILVER ARROW

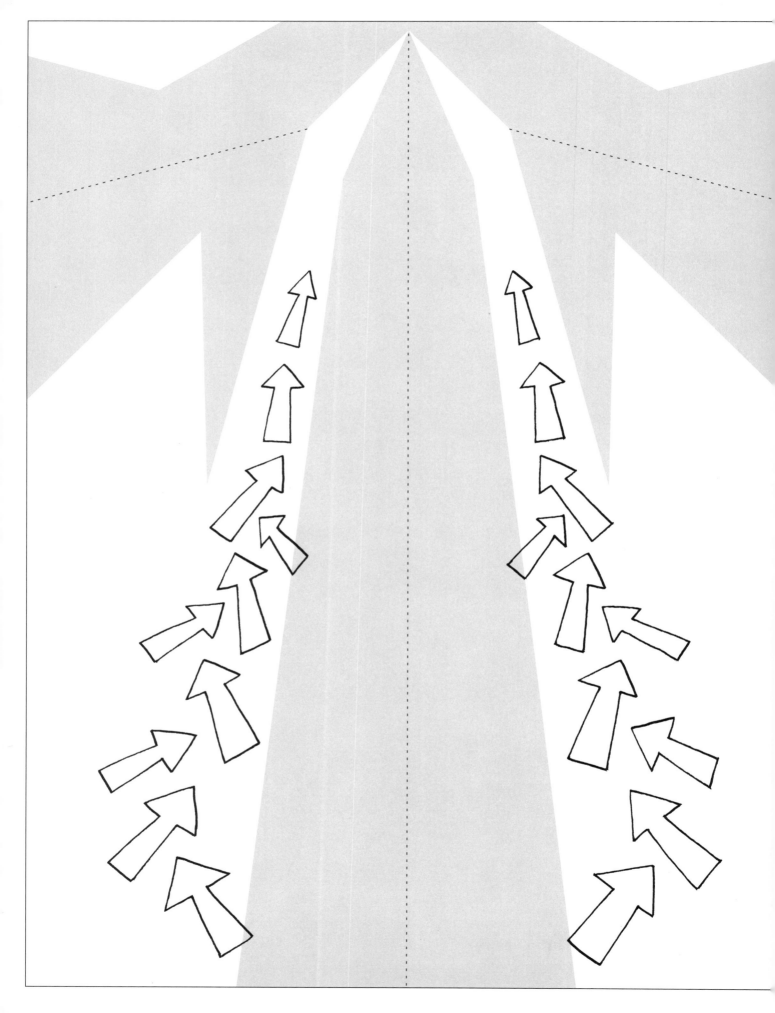

glider
front

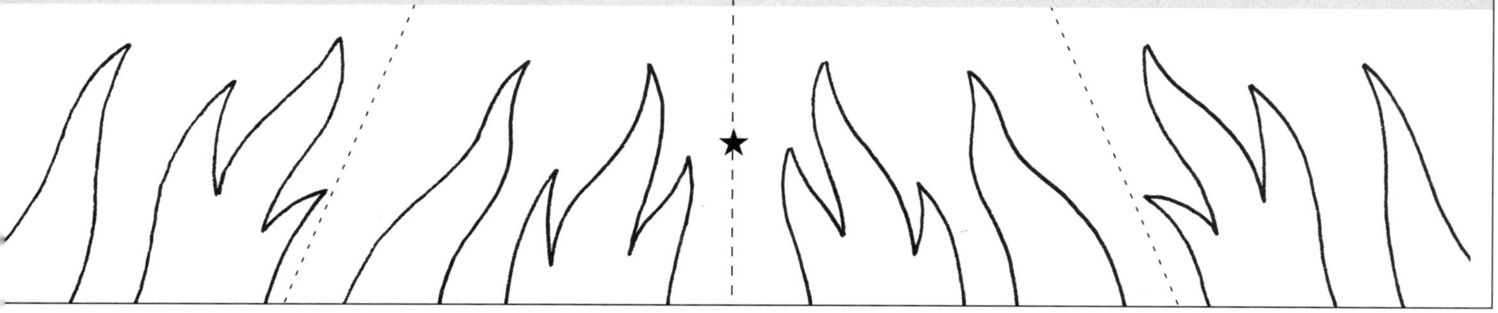

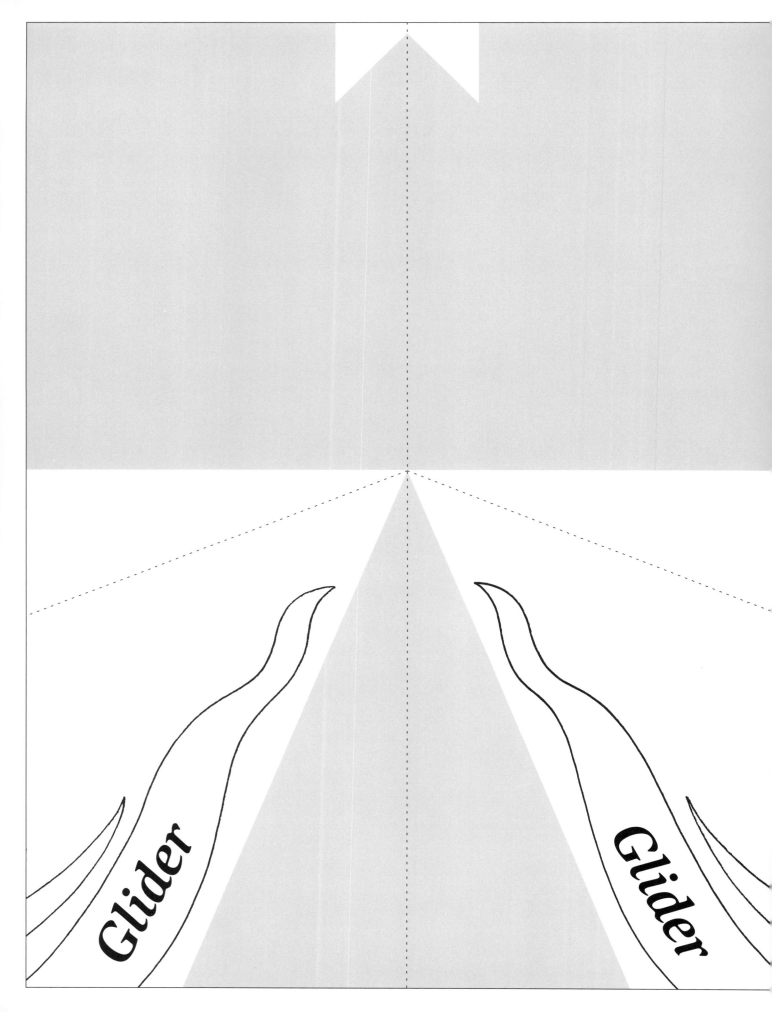

Glider

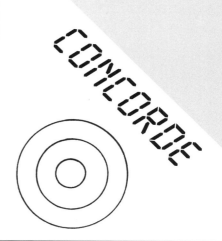

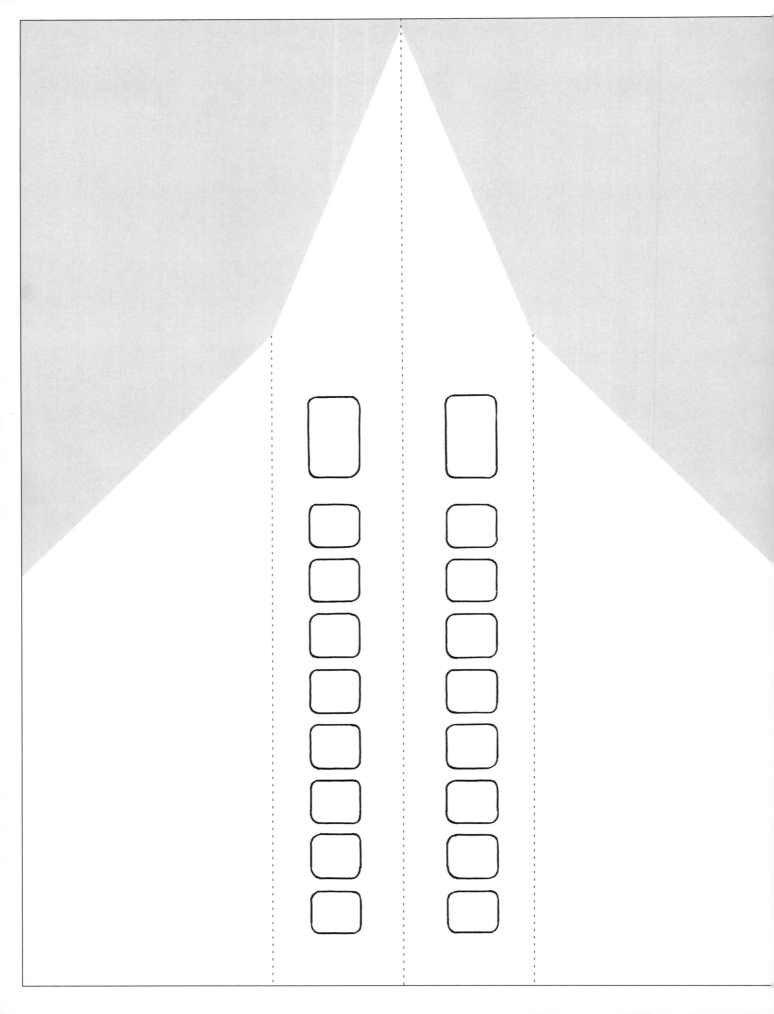

STU BBY

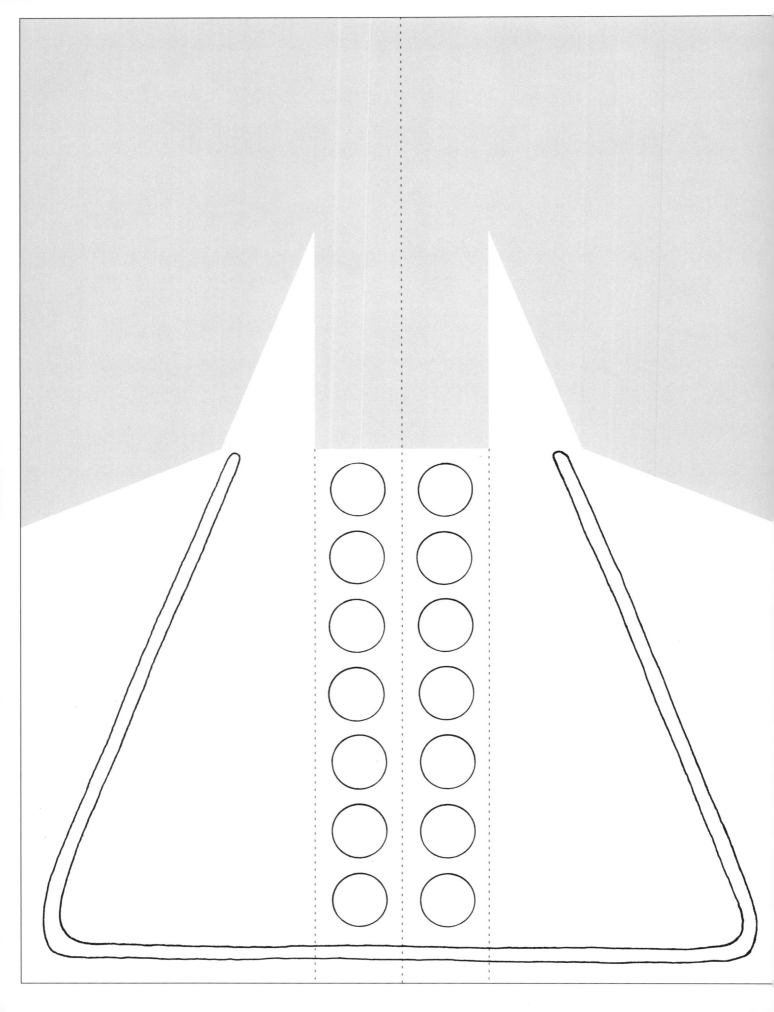

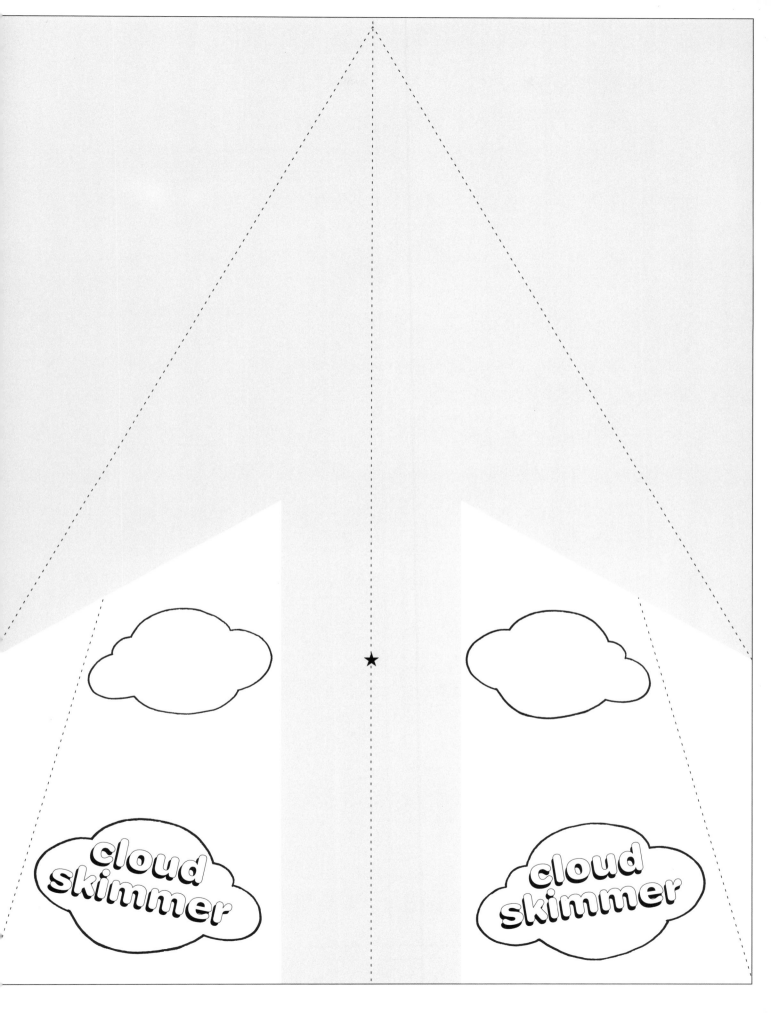

loop the looper
front

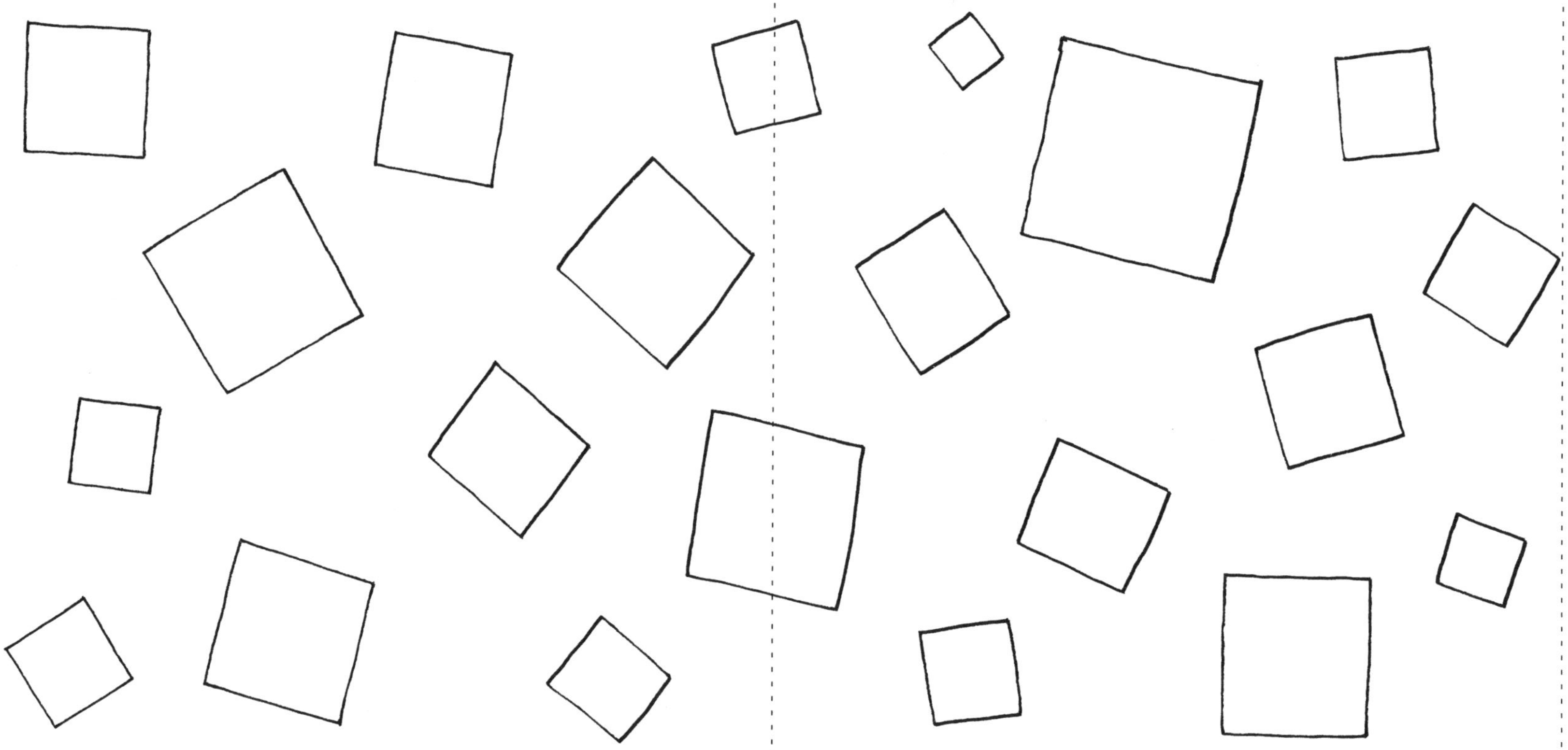

square wing
front

SQUARE WING

Cars and trucks and things that go

Using your scissors, cut along the solid lines to remove the vehicle you want to make from the book. Then colour it in following the tips on page 2. Fold along the dotted like and cut out the shape more accurately. Glue the sides together and leave to dry. The dark line shows where you cut to slot in the stand.

Large stand template

Small stand template

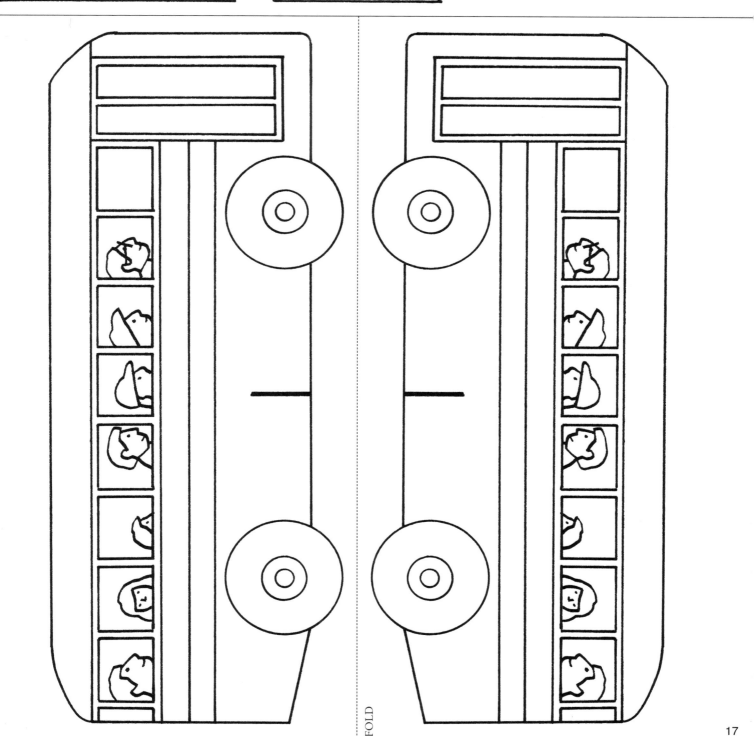

UT

Bus

FOLD

CUT

Write your name or make a design for the side of the lorry.

Lorry

CUT

FOLD

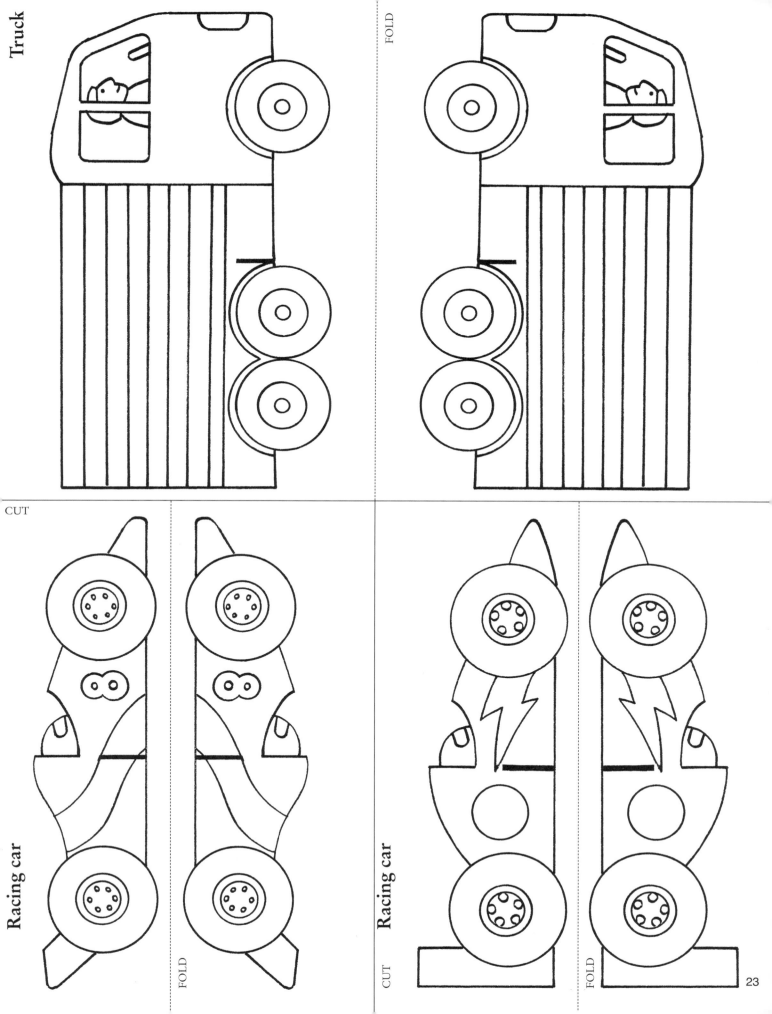

Truck

Racing car

Racing car

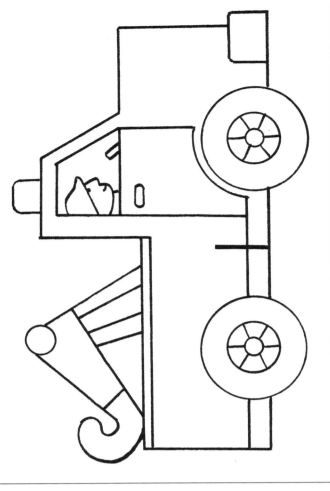
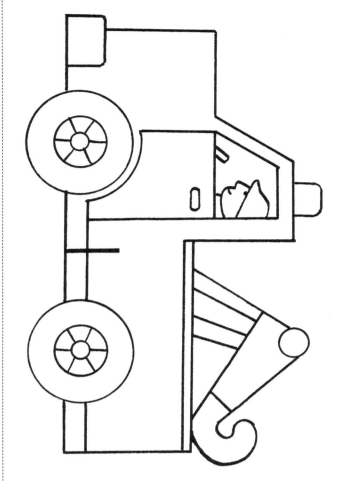

CUT

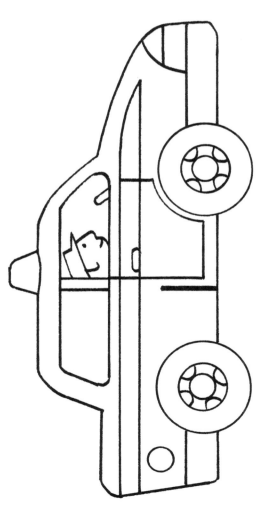
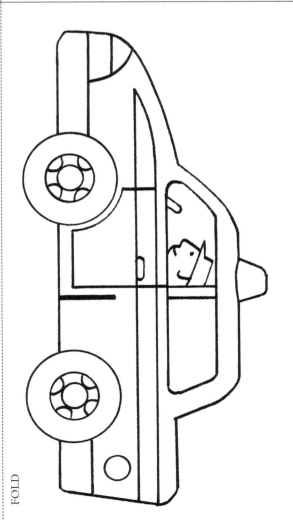

FOLD

CUT

FOLD

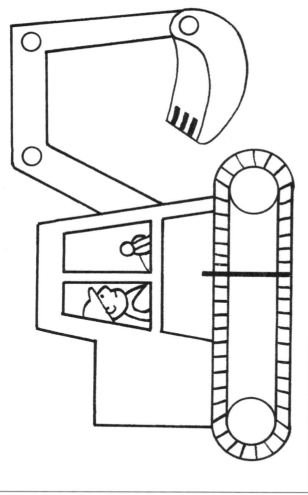

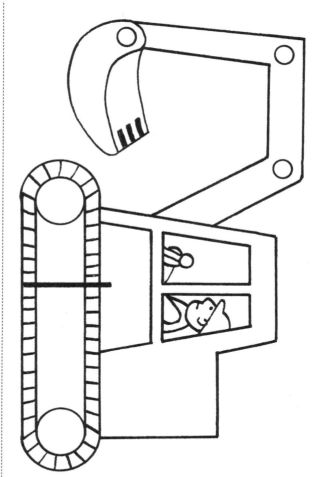

CUT

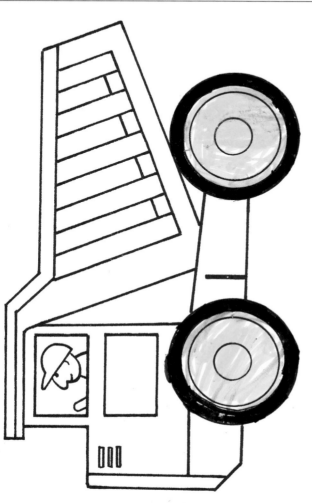

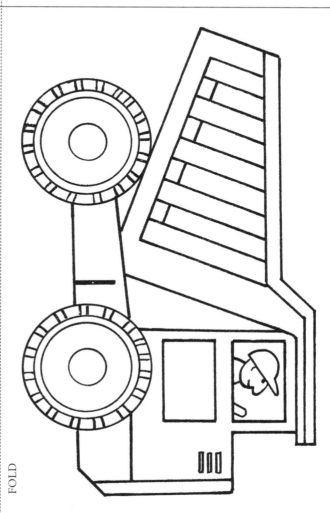

FOLD

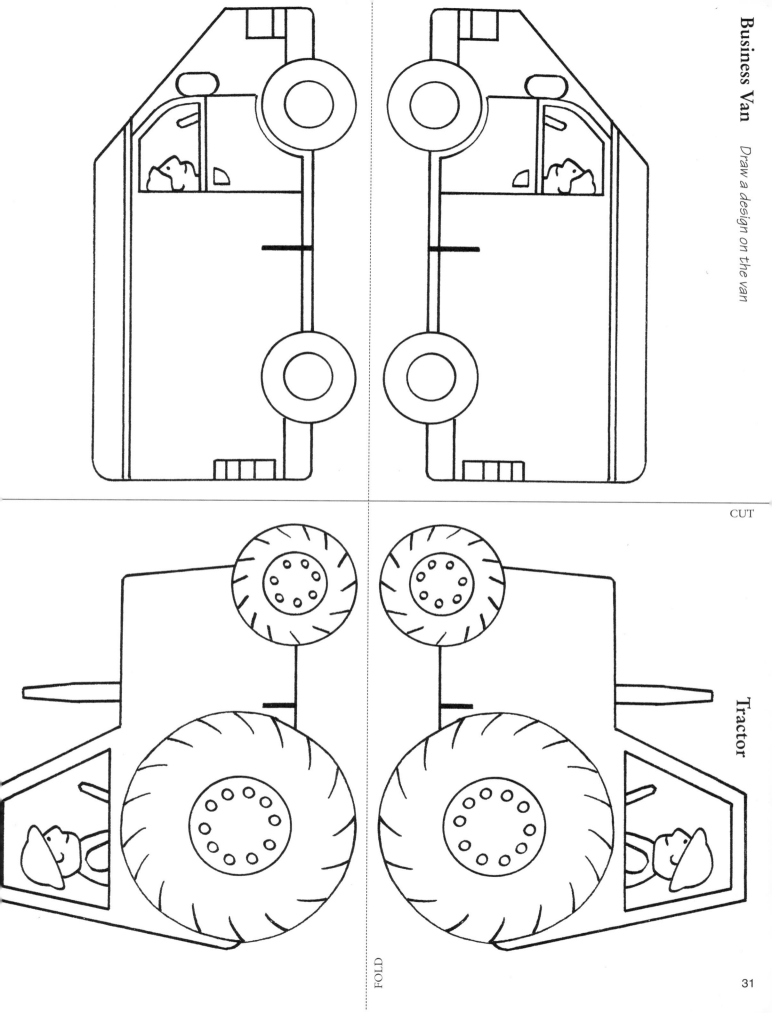

Draw a design on the van

CUT

Tractor

FOLD

Farm animals and figures

Colour in the shapes on both sides, then cut them out. (Some only have one side to colour). Cut the slots at the TOP of the legs and push them on to the animals.

Slot the wings on to the hens, ducks, etc., straight side up. Then bend them back a little.

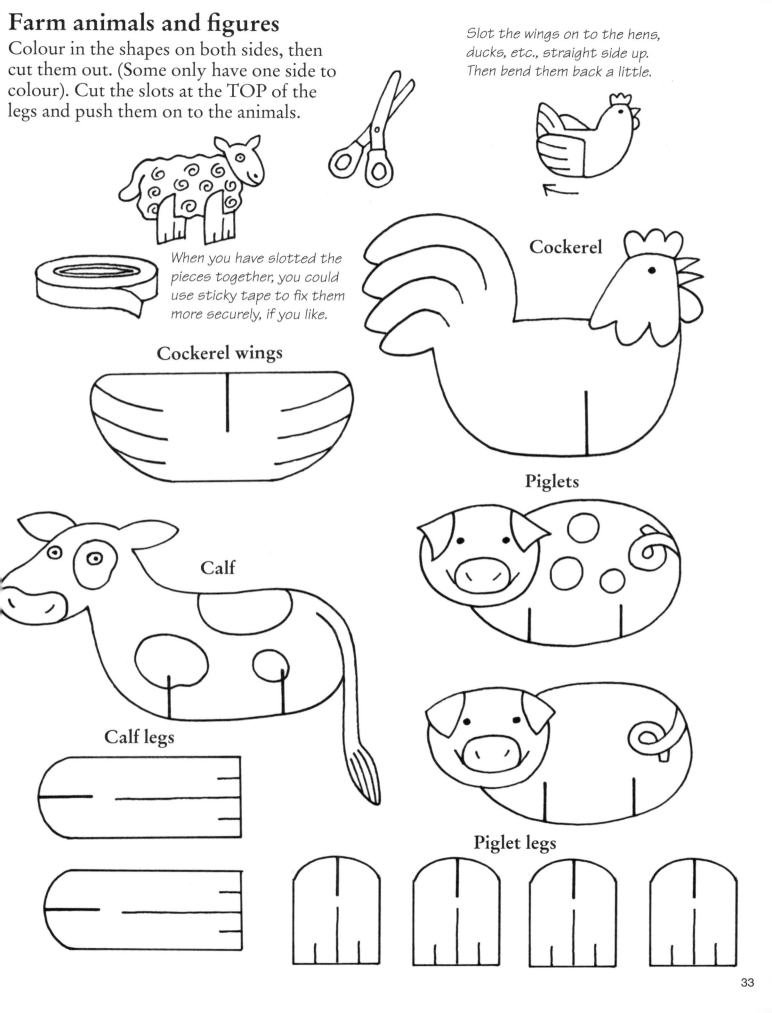

When you have slotted the pieces together, you could use sticky tape to fix them more securely, if you like.

Cockerel wings

Cockerel

Calf

Piglets

Calf legs

Piglet legs

33

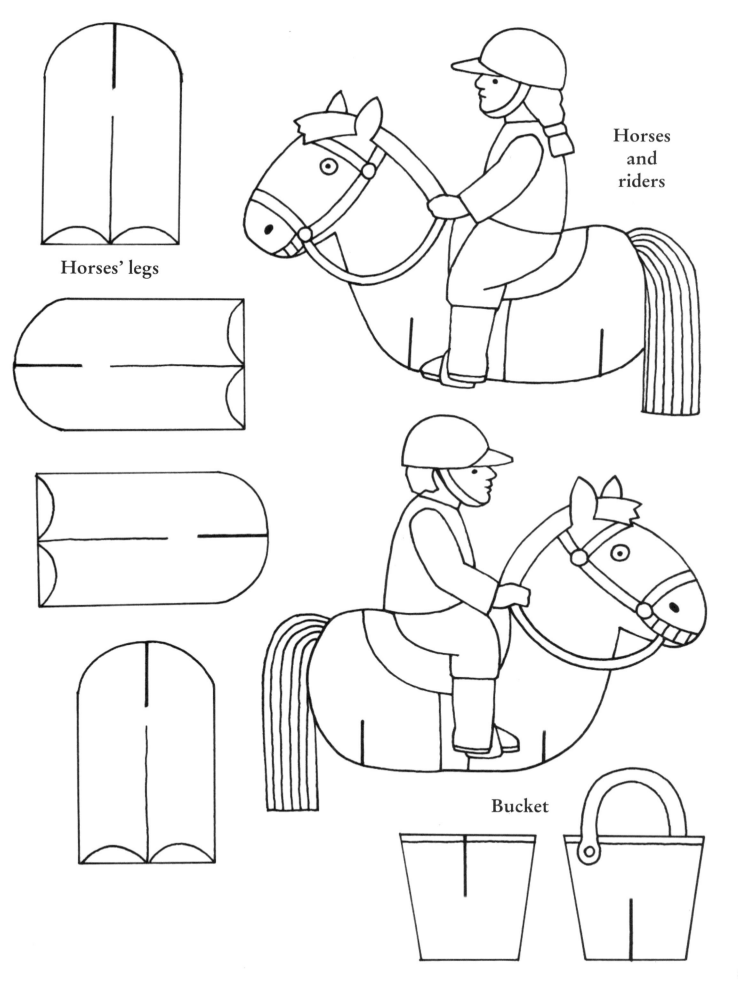

Horses' legs

Horses
and
riders

Bucket

35

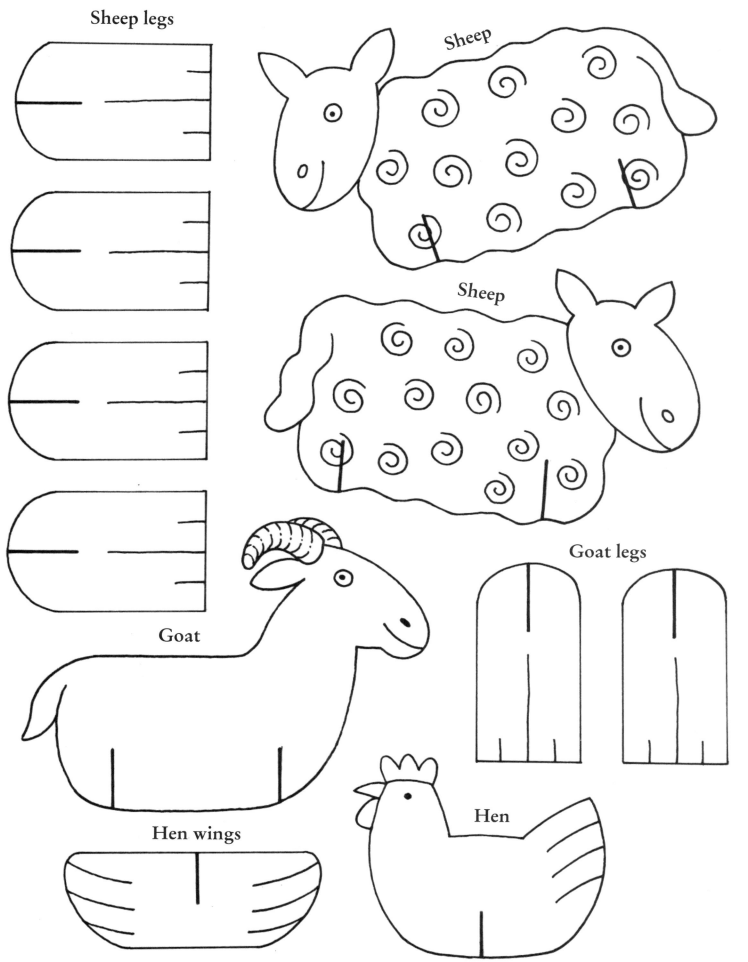

Sheep legs

Sheep

Sheep

Goat

Goat legs

Hen wings

Hen

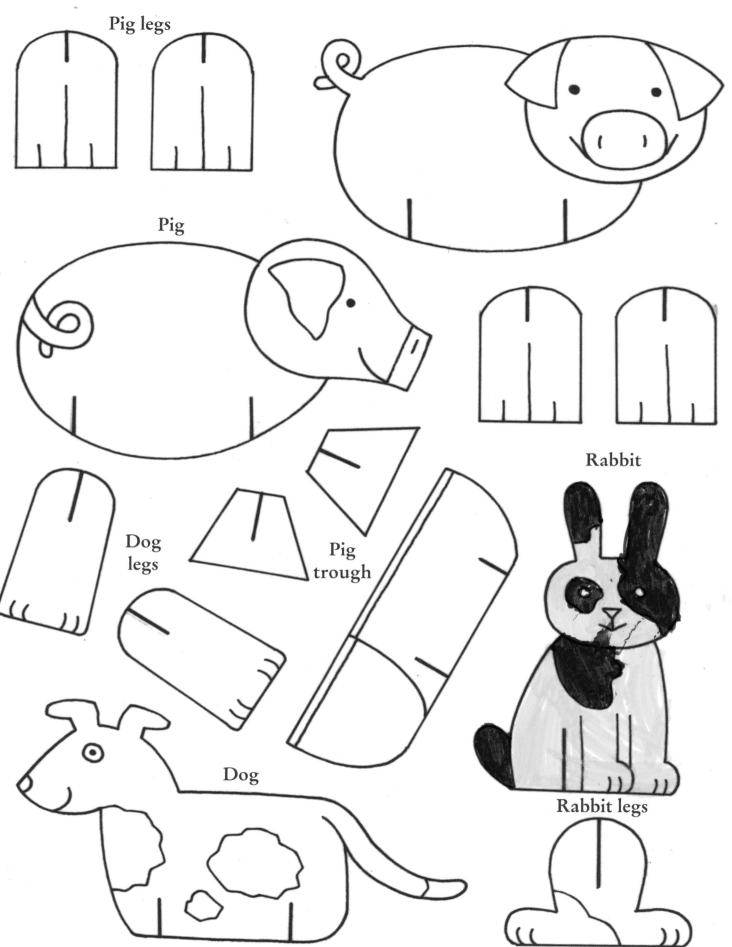

Pig legs

Pig

Dog legs

Pig trough

Rabbit

Dog

Rabbit legs

39

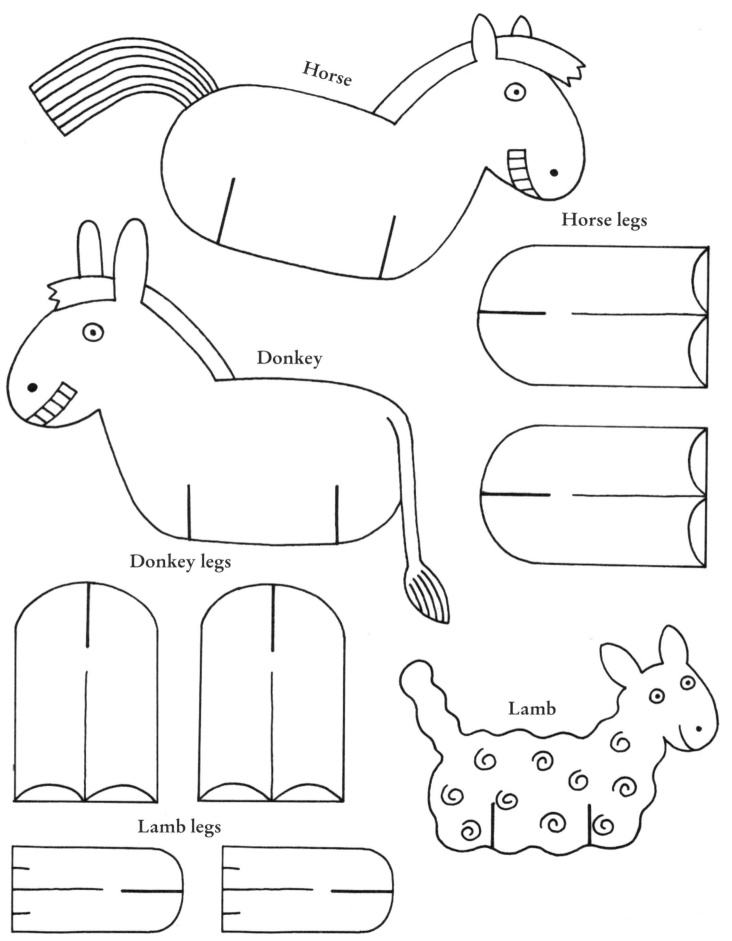

Horse

Horse legs

Donkey

Donkey legs

Lamb

Lamb legs

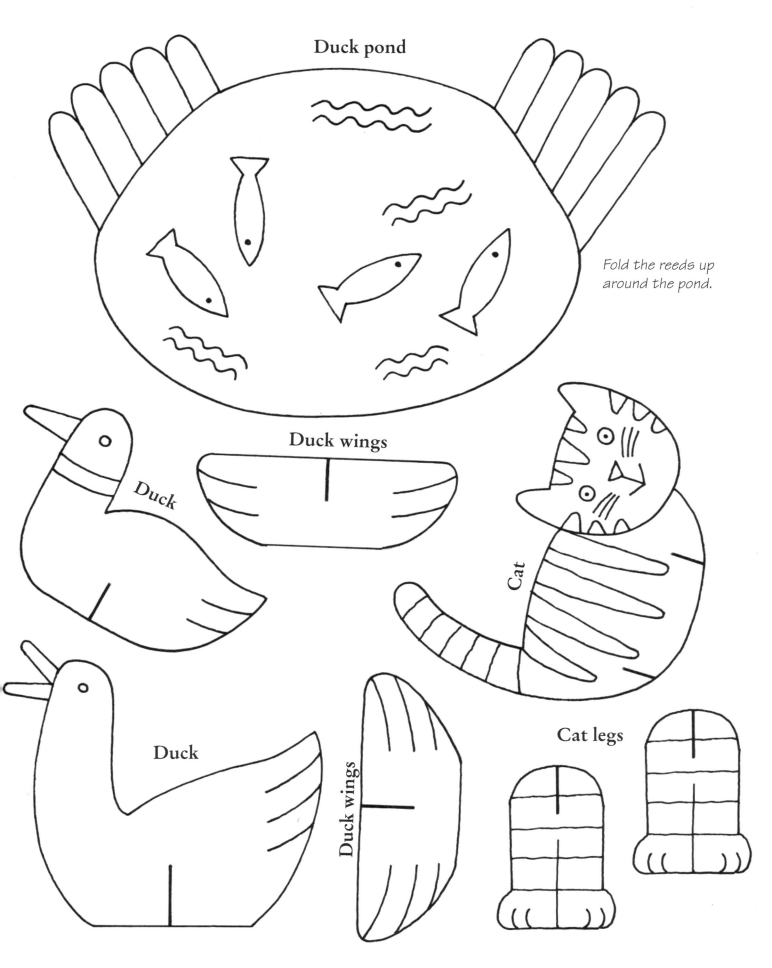

Duck pond

Fold the reeds up around the pond.

Duck wings

Duck

Cat

Duck

Duck wings

Cat legs

43

Cow

Cow legs

Cow

Cow leg

Hen wings

Hen

Farmer's wife

Farmer's children

Fold flaps back under boots.

Farmer in his tractor

Tractor stand

Dinosaurs

Colour in the dinosaurs on both sides, then cut them out. Cut the slots in the bodies and at the TOP of the legs. Then push the legs on to the bodies and stand them up.

Some legs have dotted lines. Before you slot these on to the bodies, fold along the lines and bend the legs forward, as shown here.

Pachycephalosaur

Triceratops skeleton

First cut the slots where marked. Then colour between the bones in black.

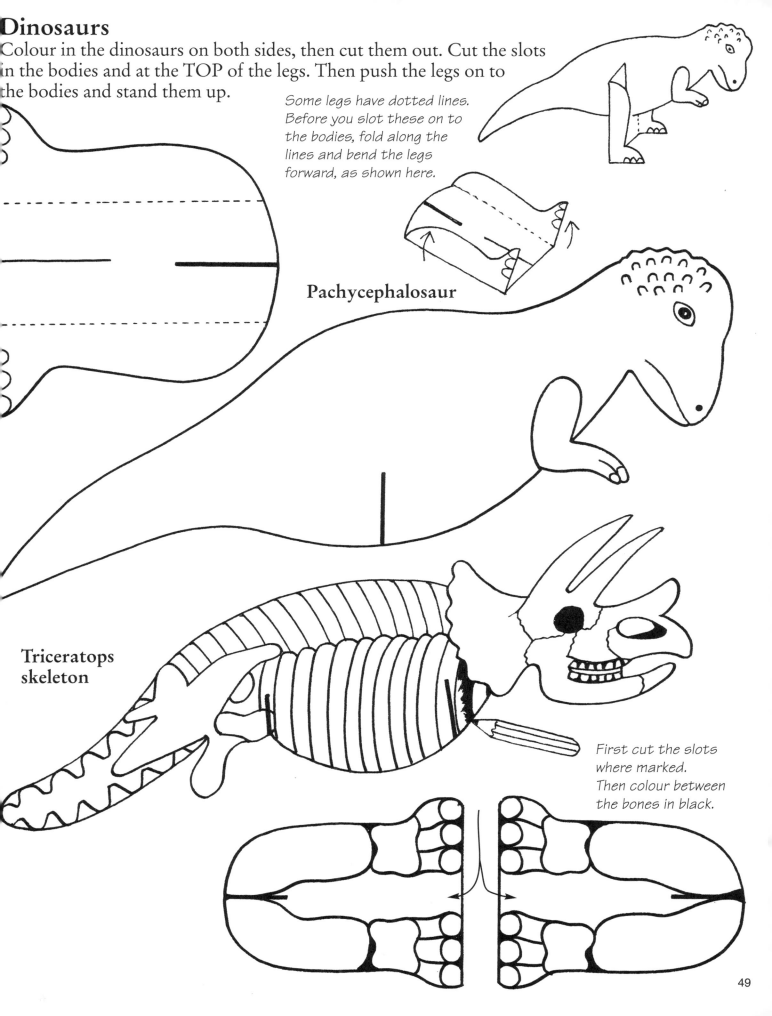

49

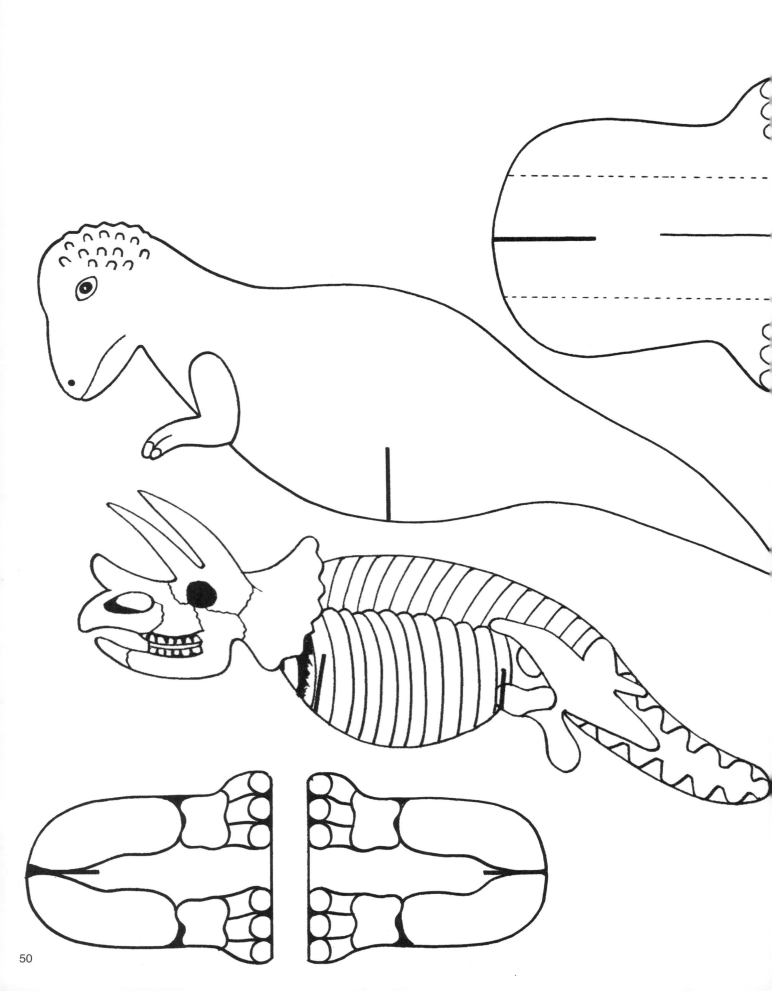

Fold into zigzag.

Vegetation

Vegetation

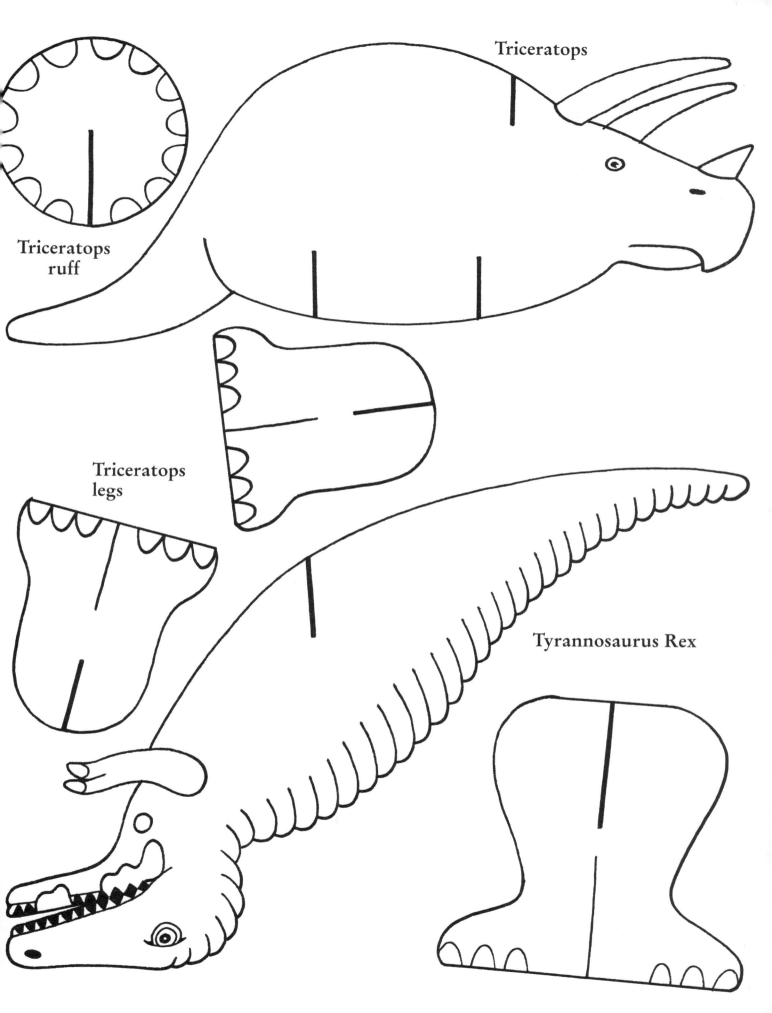

Triceratops

Triceratops
ruff

Triceratops
legs

Tyrannosaurus Rex

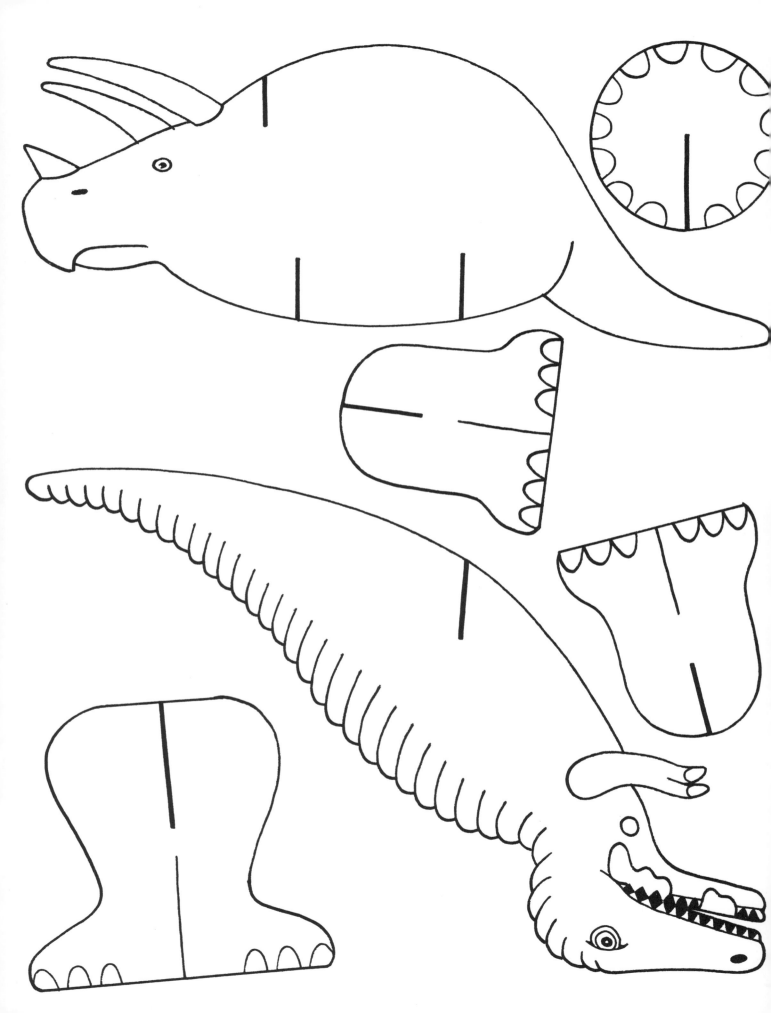

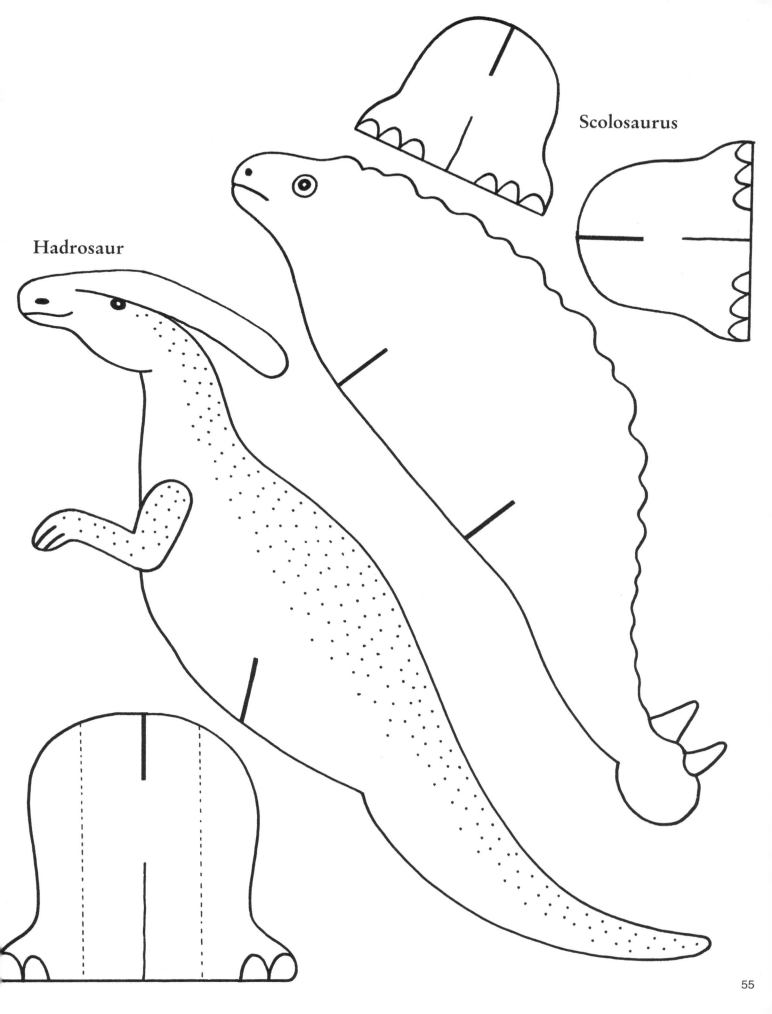

Scolosaurus

Hadrosaur

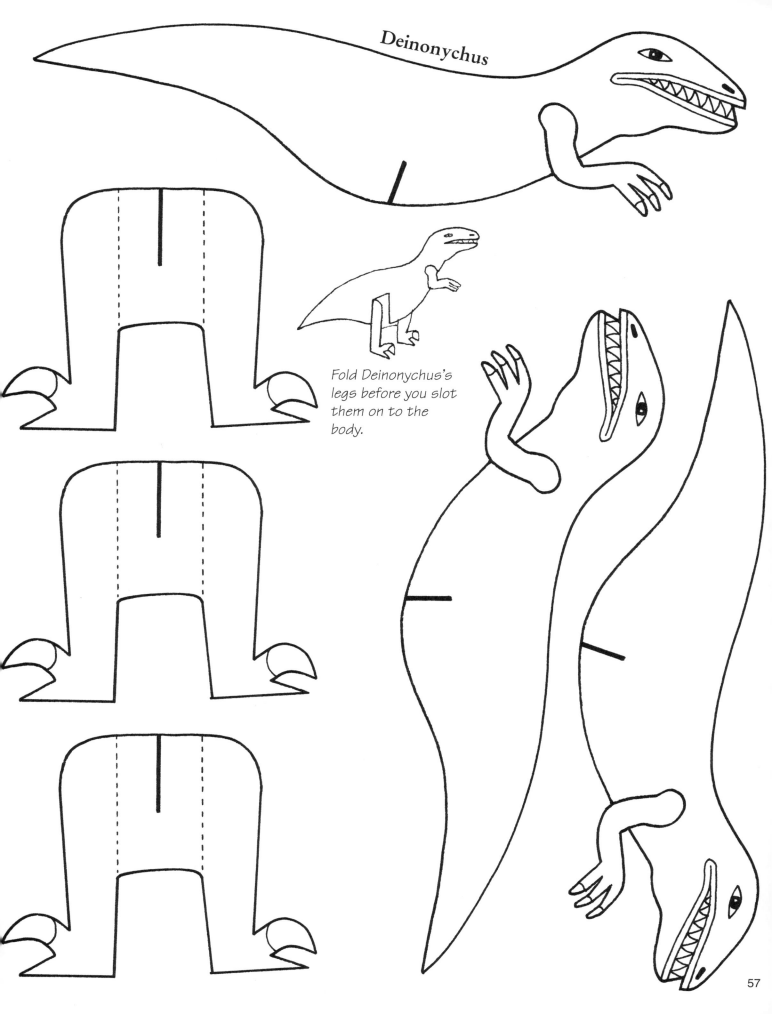

Deinonychus

Fold Deinonychus's legs before you slot them on to the body.

57

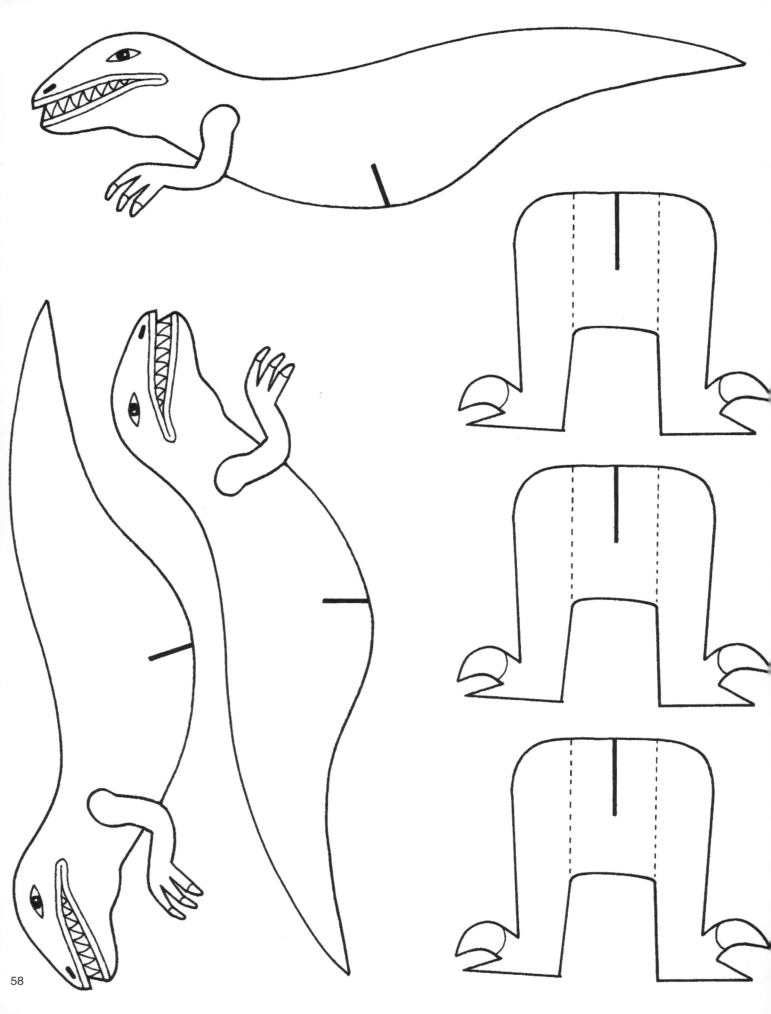

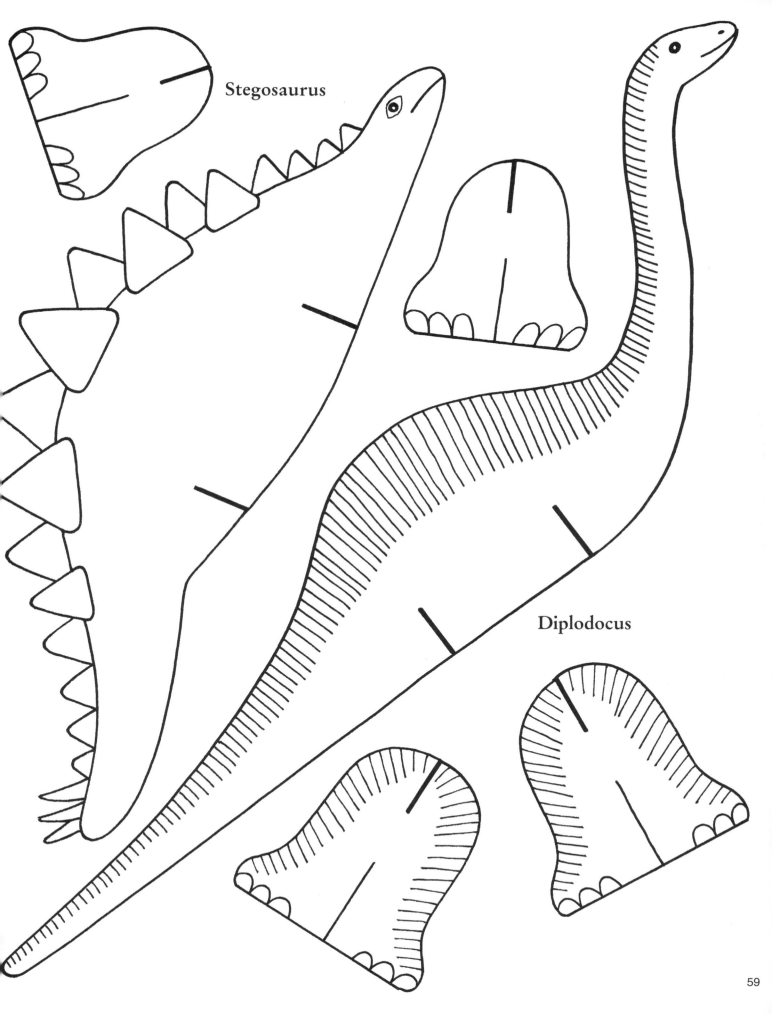

Stegosaurus

Diplodocus

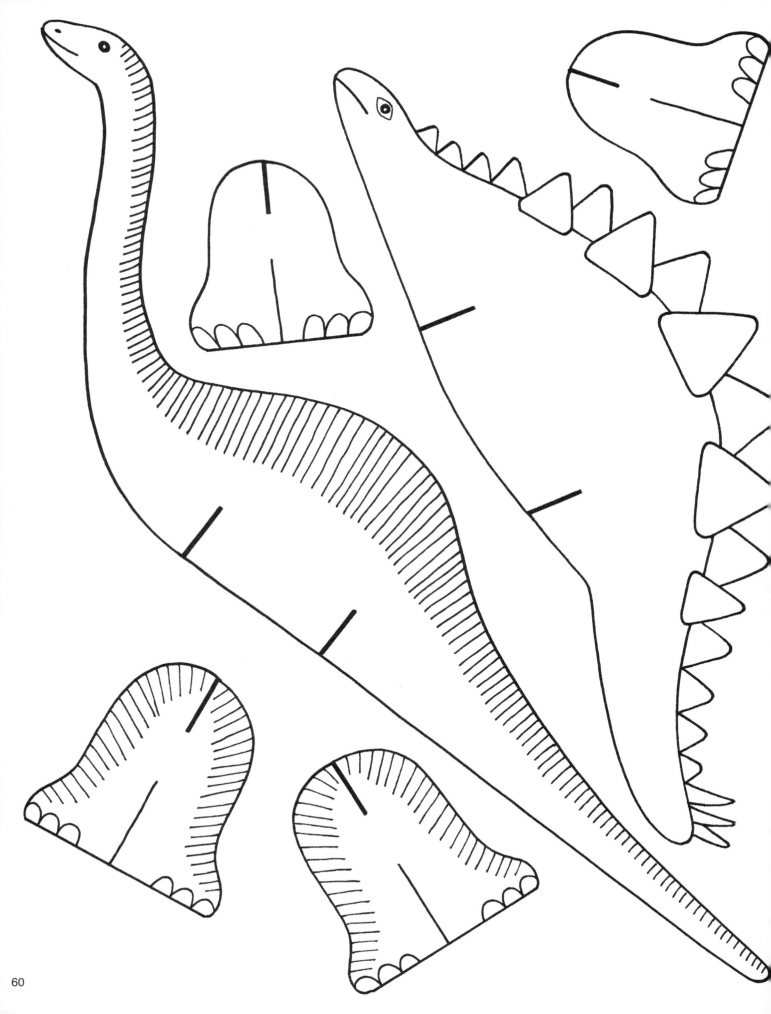

Dinosaur nests

Colour in and cut out.

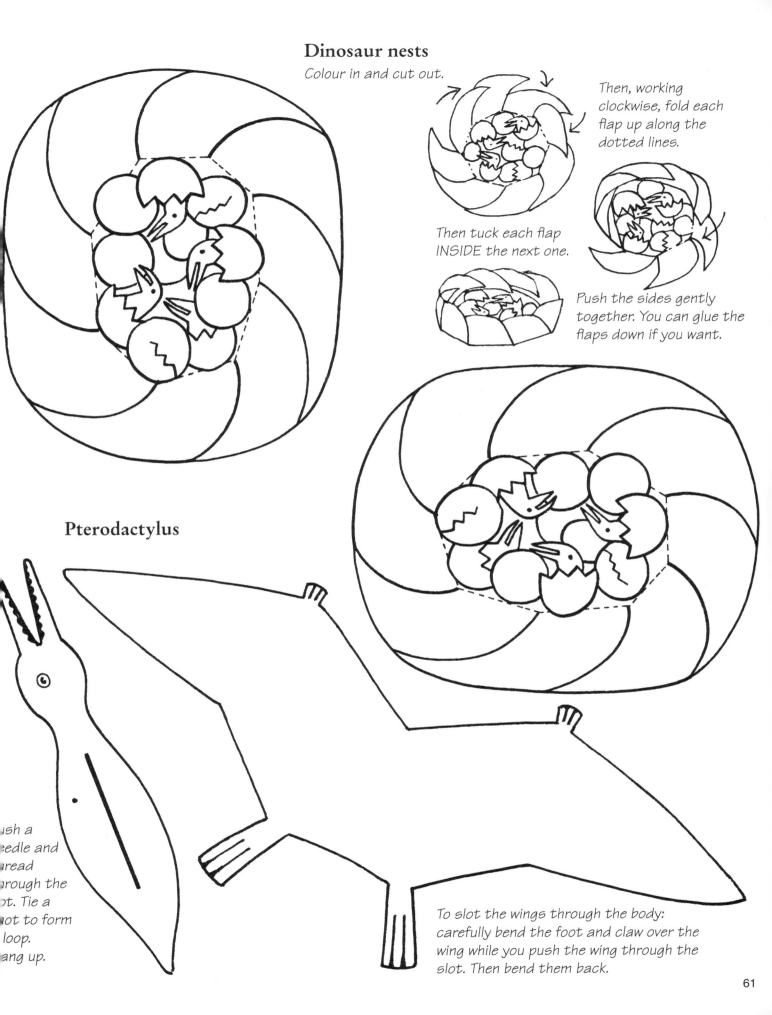

Then, working clockwise, fold each flap up along the dotted lines.

Then tuck each flap INSIDE the next one.

Push the sides gently together. You can glue the flaps down if you want.

Pterodactylus

ush a
eedle and
hread
rough the
ot. Tie a
ot to form
 loop.
ang up.

To slot the wings through the body: carefully bend the foot and claw over the wing while you push the wing through the slot. Then bend them back.

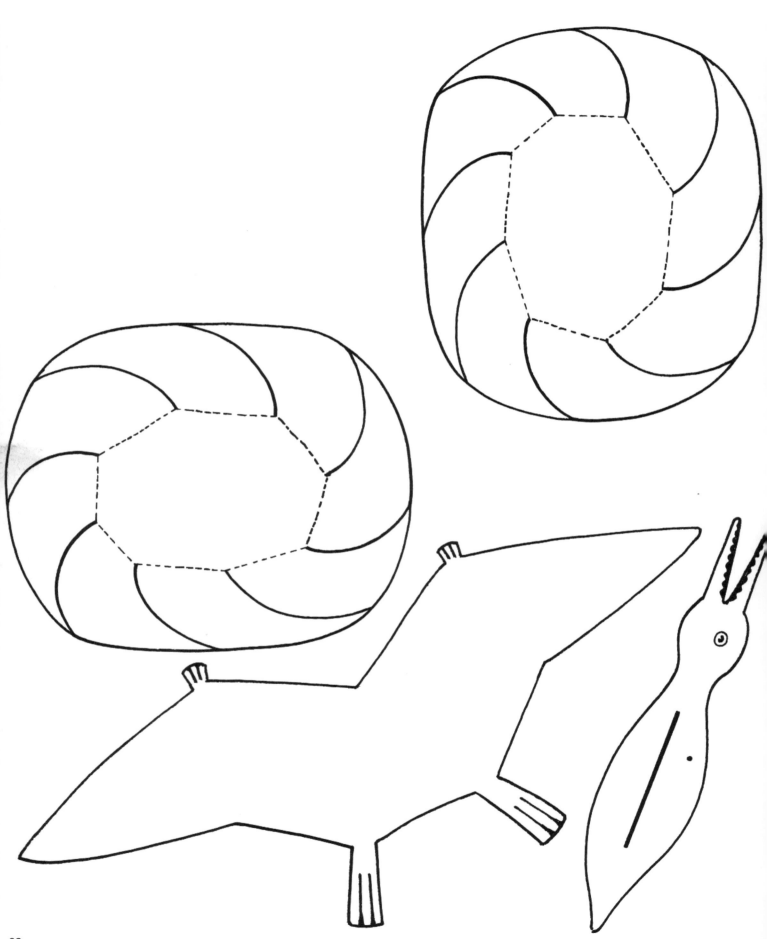

Volcano

Colour in and cut out. Glue
along the flap where marked.
Bend the shape to form a cone.
Hold it together until it is dry.

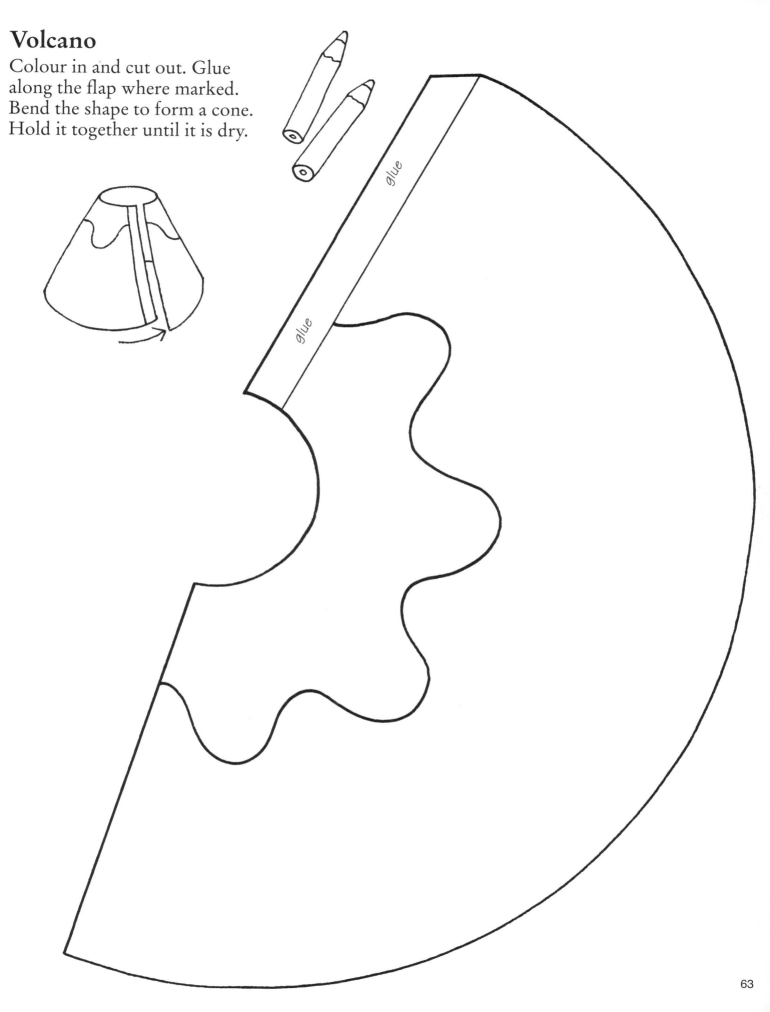

glue

glue

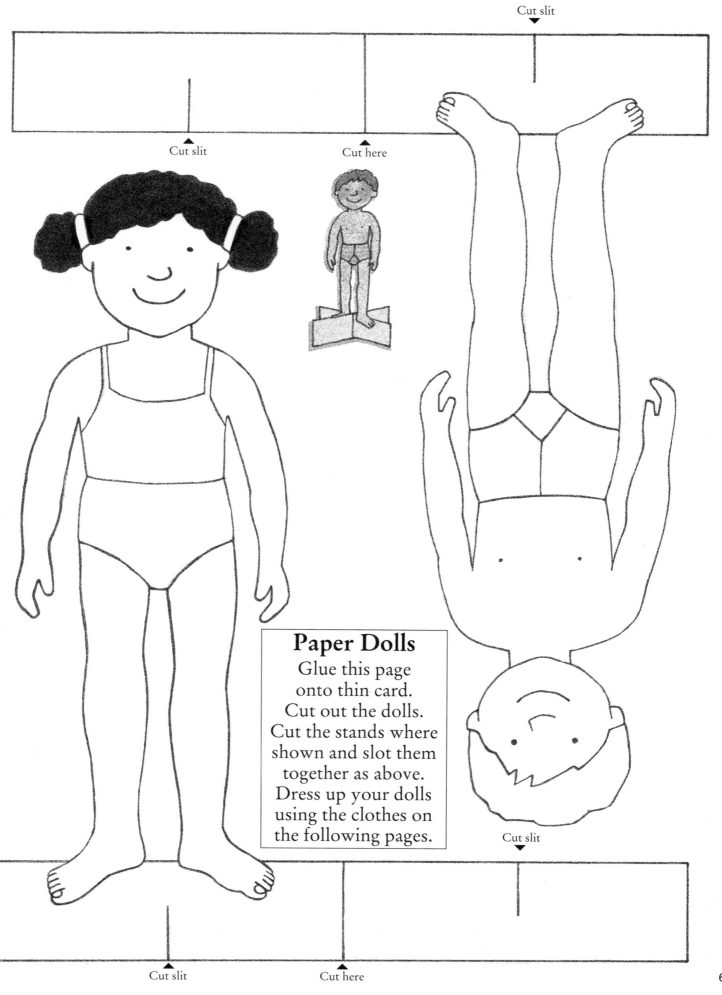

Cut slit

Cut slit

Cut here

Paper Dolls
Glue this page
onto thin card.
Cut out the dolls.
Cut the stands where
shown and slot them
together as above.
Dress up your dolls
using the clothes on
the following pages.

Cut slit

Cut slit

Cut here

Sports

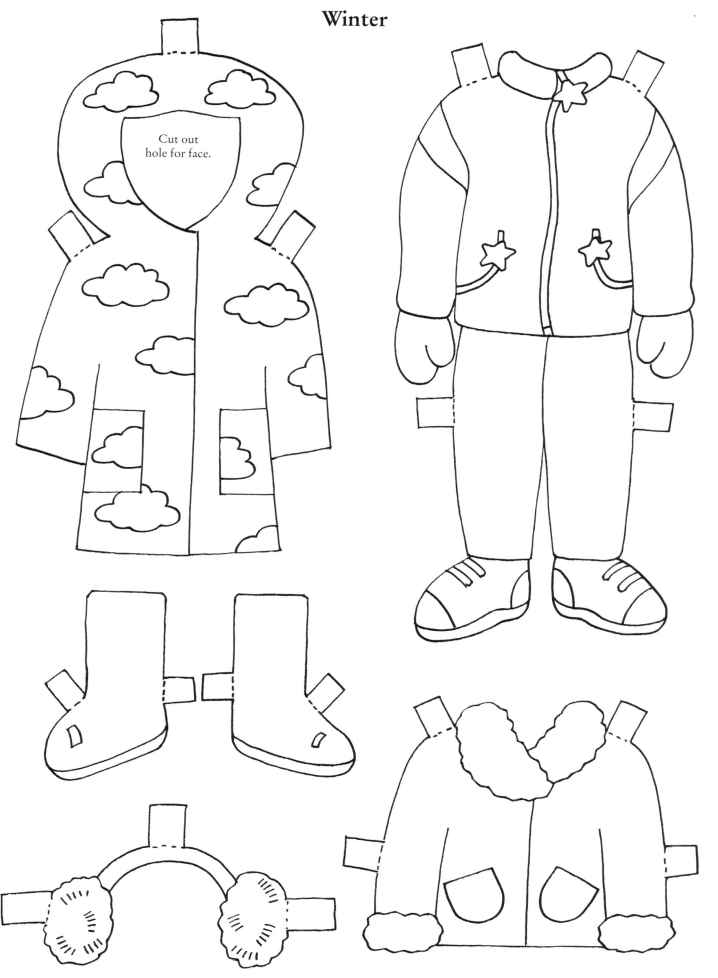

Cut out hole for face.

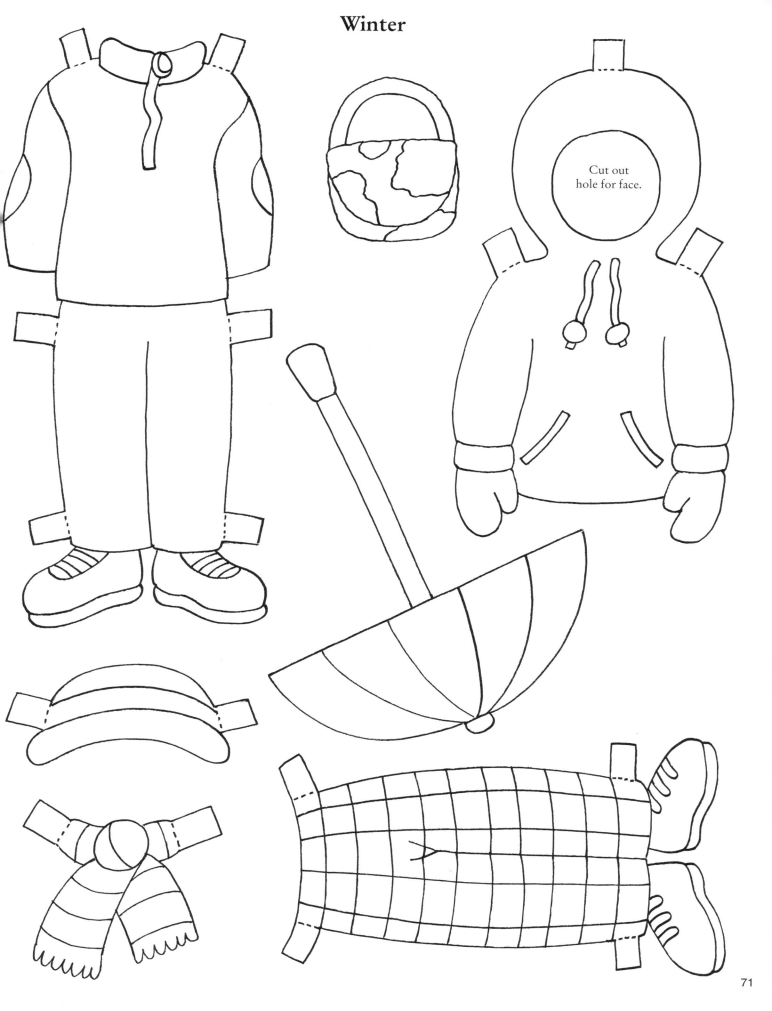

Cut out
hole for face.

Dressing up

Cut carefully between tabs and wings.

Parties

Summer

Bedtime

Gifts and Decorations

Colour both sides. Cut them out and thread wool through the holes to hang them up.

Glue wing here.

Dove card

Cut the dove card from this page. Fold it and colour it in, except for the wing area. Cut out the wings below. Colour them in, fold and glue them on to the dove where marked.

Three mini cards

I ♥ you

Glue area.
Do not colour.

84

Necklaces

Colour and cut out the pieces.
Thread with a needle and wool
through the centres. Knot the ends.

Thread the leaves through the dots.

85

Bookmarks Colour them in and cut them out. Write messages on the other side.

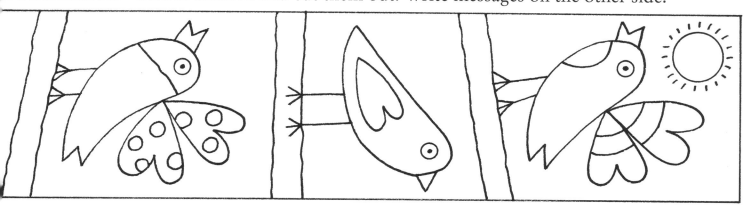

Colour in and write your message.

Frame

Colour the front of the frame around the heart. Cut out the centre heart shape.

Fold the whole page in half horizontally. Position your photo or picture under the heart so that it shows through. Glue the photo or picture in place. Then glue the folded page together.

Cut along the solid diagonal line on the back of the frame and fold along the dotted line.

Fold the frame again and glue it together, avoiding the hole left by the flap. Stand it up, using the flap.

Three heart baskets

Decorate and colour these in. Cut out and fold along the dotted lines.

Put glue on the flaps. Press together.

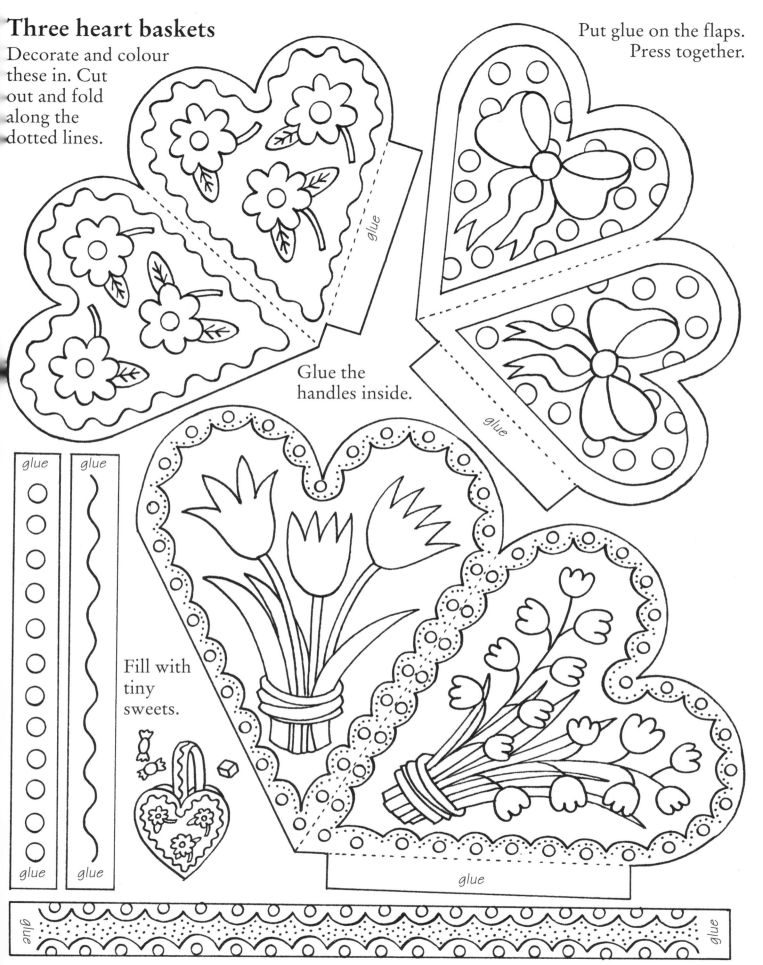

Glue the handles inside.

Fill with tiny sweets.

glue

glue

glue

glue

glue

glue

glue

glue

glue

glue

Forget
me not

I miss you!

Roses are red
Violets are blue
Sugar is sweet
And so are you.

She loves me,
she loves me not.

Things that live under the sea
Colour in the shapes on both sides, then cut them out.

Whale

When a shape has a large black dot marked, use a needle and thread to pierce through it, so you can hang the creature up.

Lobster

Giant clam

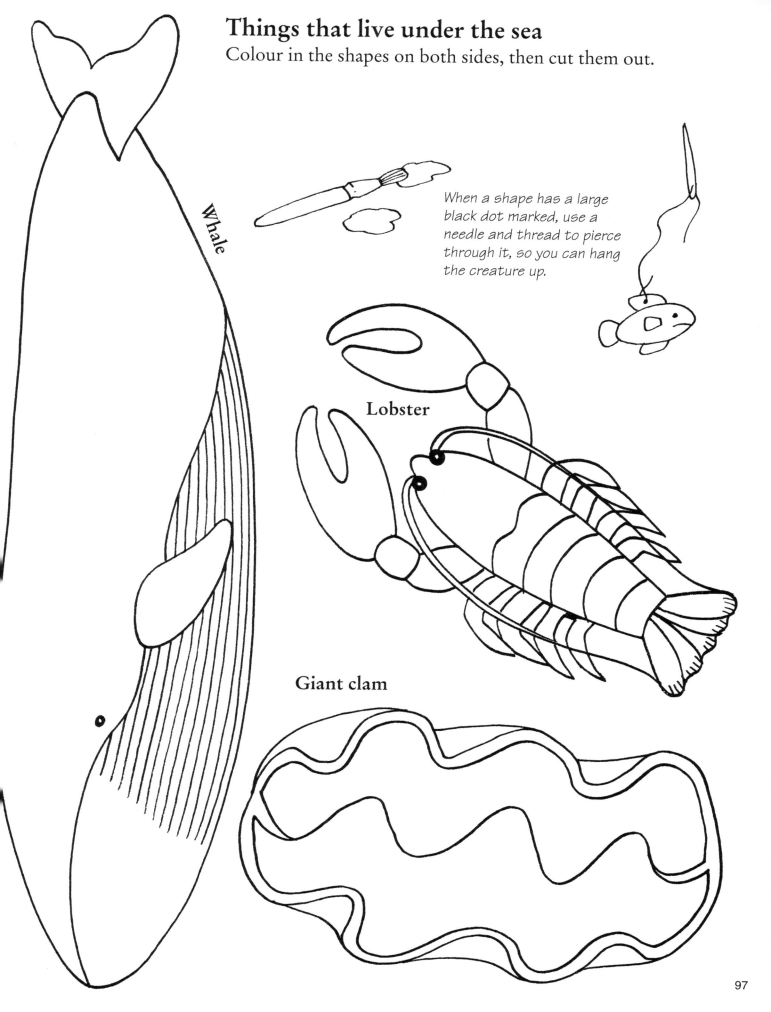

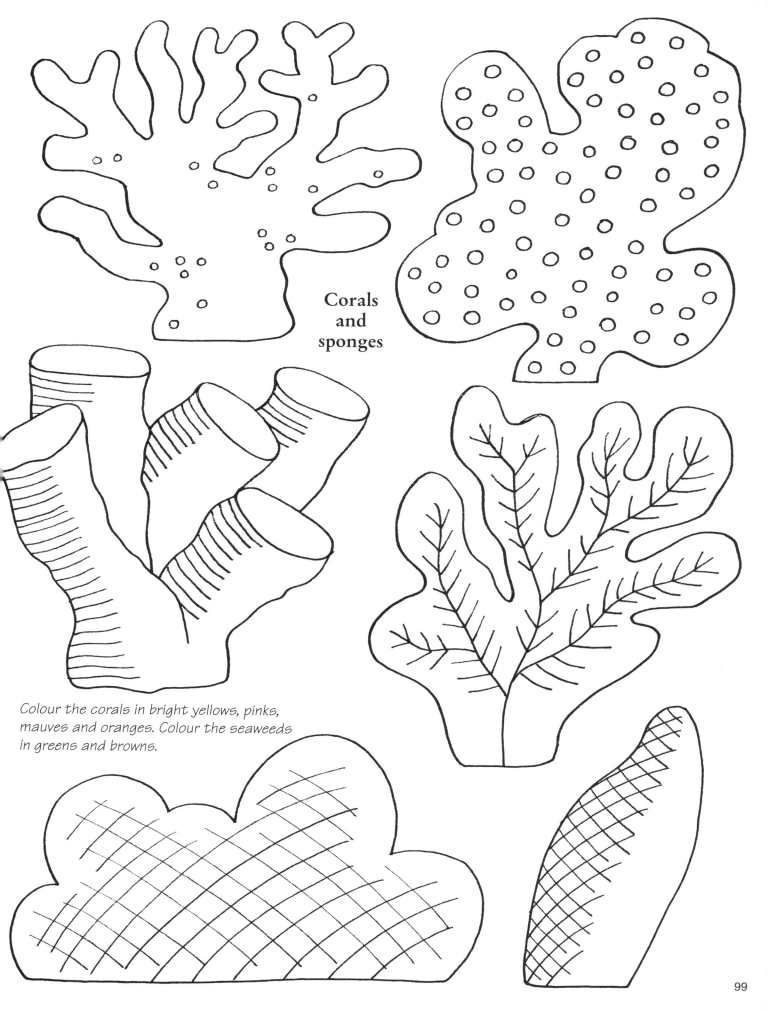

Corals
and
sponges

Colour the corals in bright yellows, pinks,
mauves and oranges. Colour the seaweeds
in greens and browns.

Hermit crab

Swordfish

Turtle

Sea slug

Cucumber

Sea snail

Electric eel

Sharks

Angel fish

Piranha

Common sunstar

103

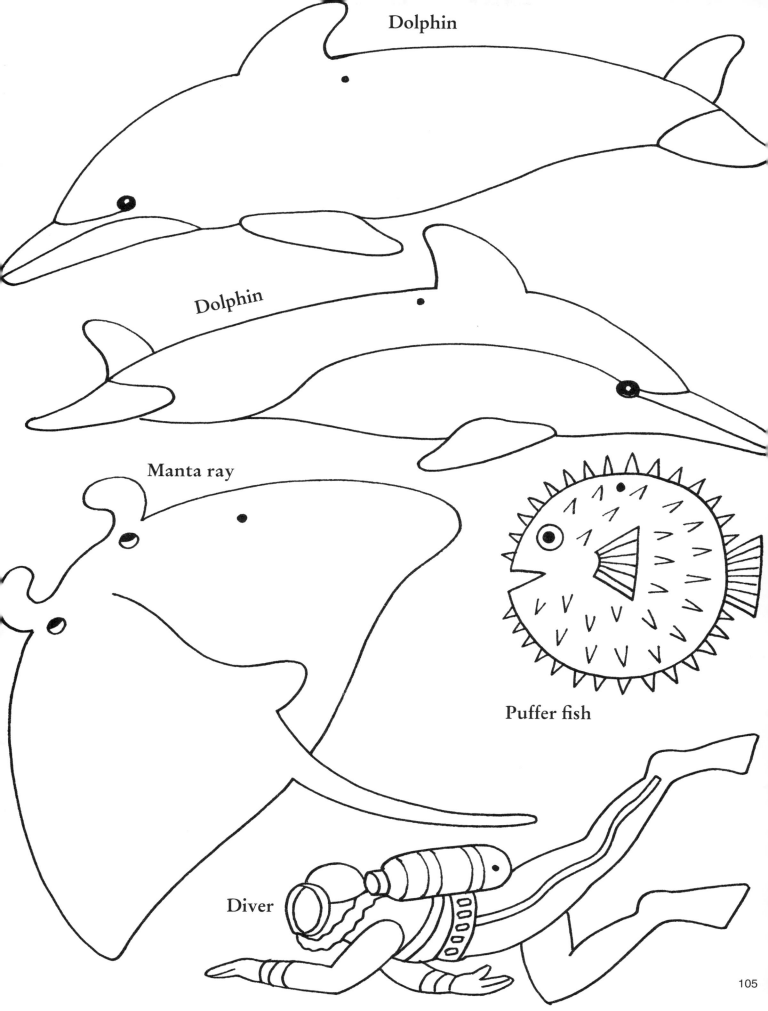

Dolphin

Dolphin

Manta ray

Puffer fish

Diver

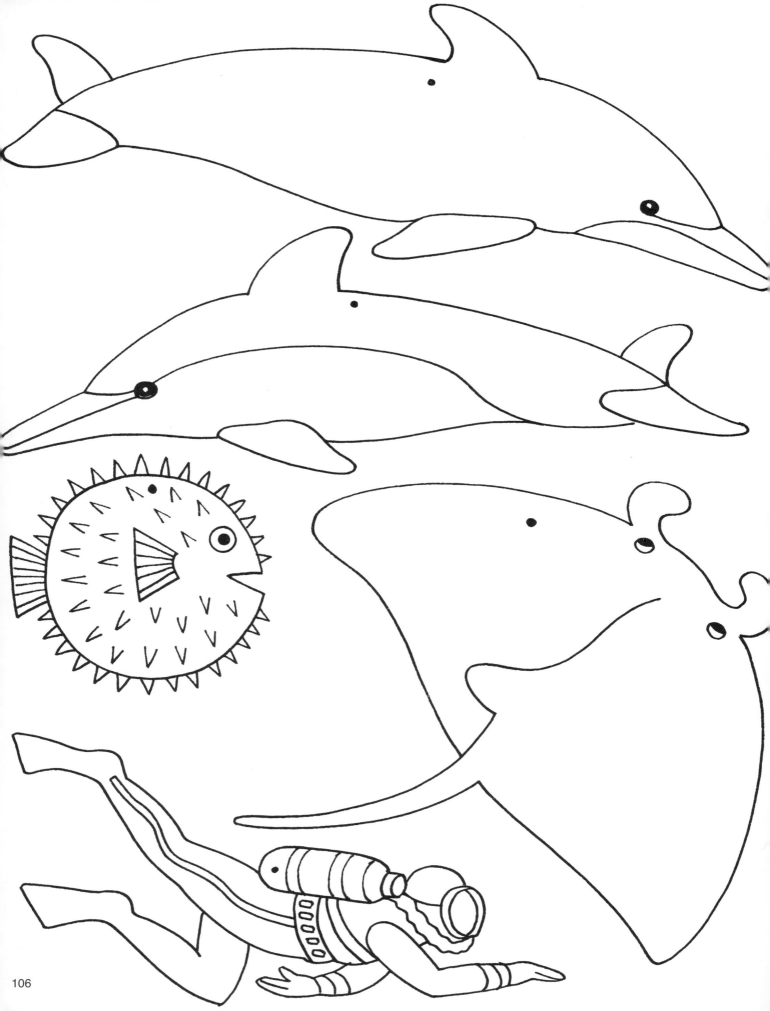

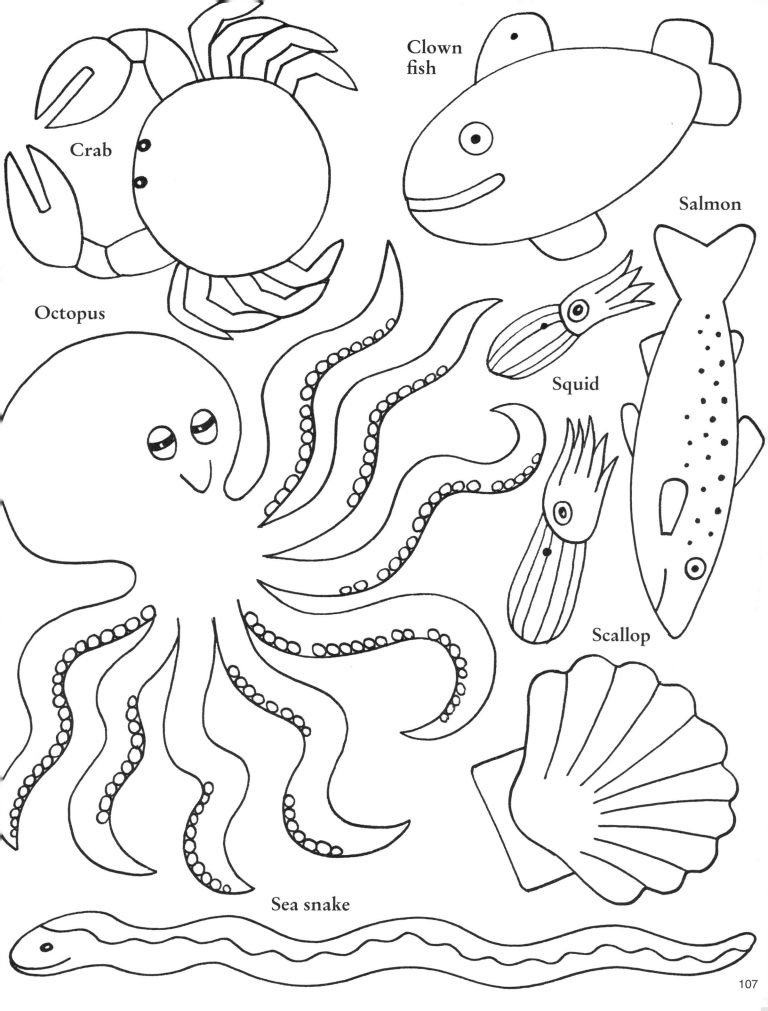

Crab

Clown
fish

Salmon

Octopus

Squid

Scallop

Sea snake

Starfish

Shrimp

Tropical fish

Shrimp

Seahorse

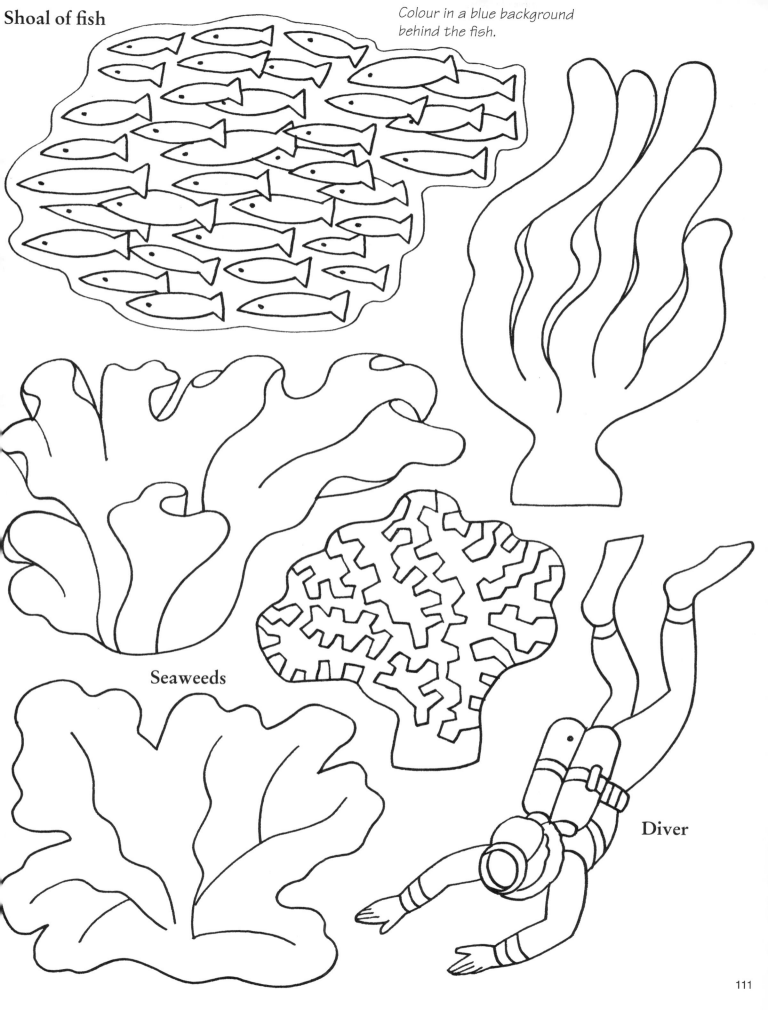

Shoal of fish

Colour in a blue background behind the fish.

Seaweeds

Diver

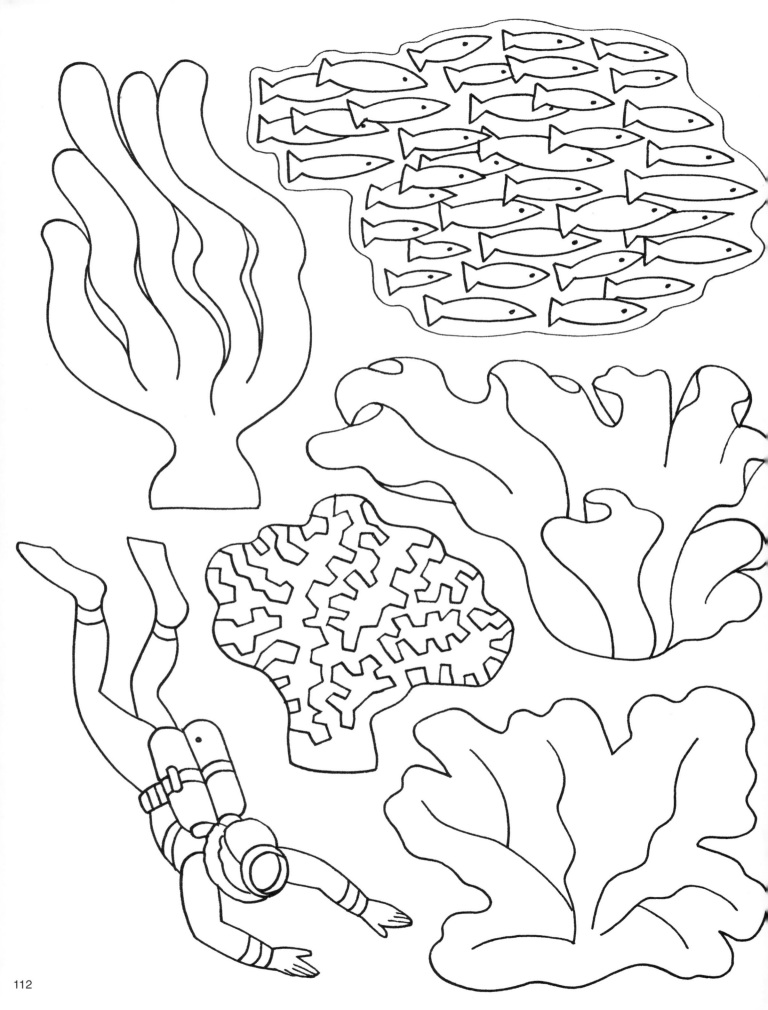

Wild animals and figures

Colour in the shapes on both sides, then cut them out.
Cut the slots in the bodies and at the TOP of the legs,
then push the legs on to the bodies. Stand them up.

When you have slotted the pieces together, you can fix them more securely with sticky tape, if you like.

Zebra

Zebra legs

Zebra legs

Zebra

Zebra legs

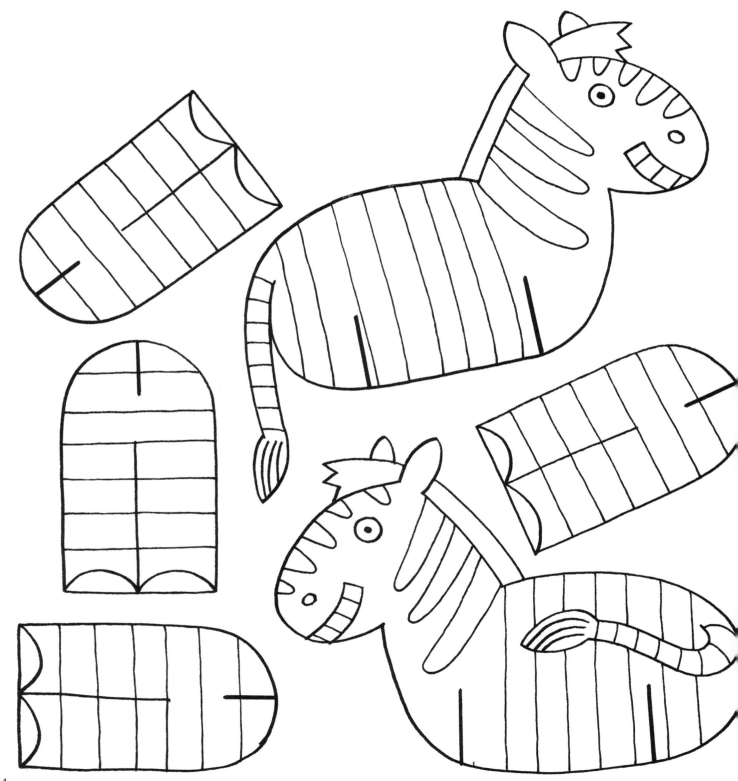

Kangaroo legs

Kangaroo

Parrot

If you want to perch
a koala or parrot on
thicker card, cut the
slit a bit wider, to fit.

Parrot

Koalas

Kangaroo
and legs

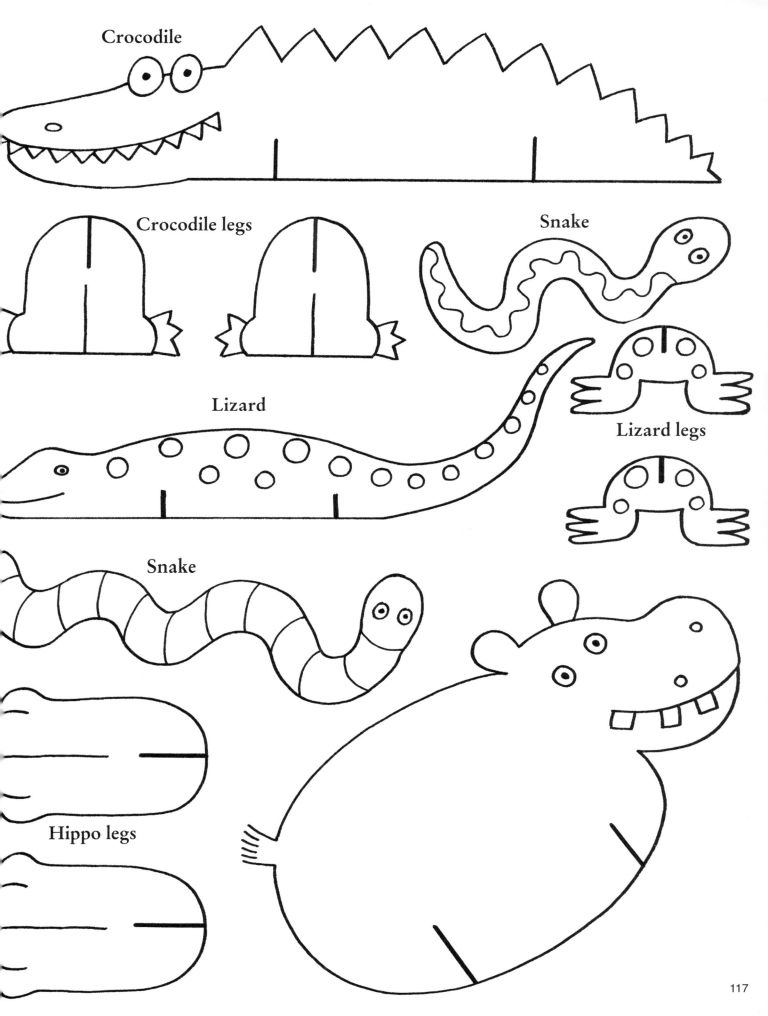

Crocodile

Crocodile legs

Snake

Lizard

Lizard legs

Snake

Hippo legs

117

People on safari

To stand the people up, fold back the tab under their shoes.

119

Monkeys

Hang them by their tails on vines.

Gorilla rear legs

Gorilla front legs

Gorilla

Lion legs

Lion

Tiger

Tiger legs

Camel

Camel legs

Gazelle

Gazelle legs

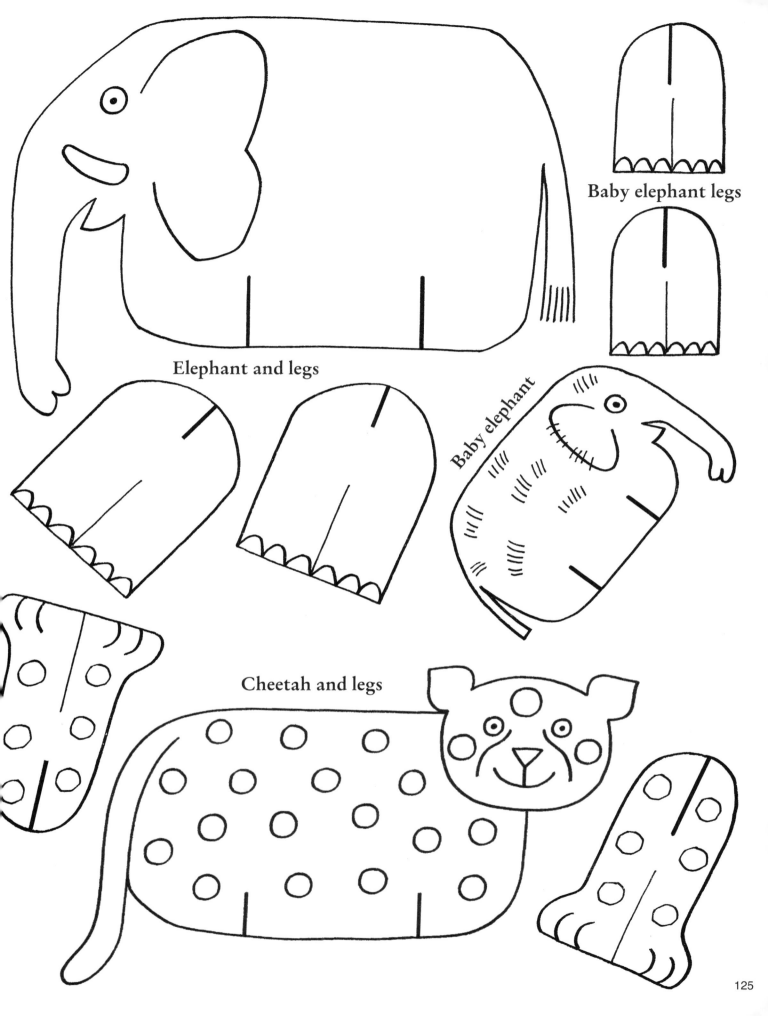

Baby elephant legs

Elephant and legs

Baby elephant

Cheetah and legs

125

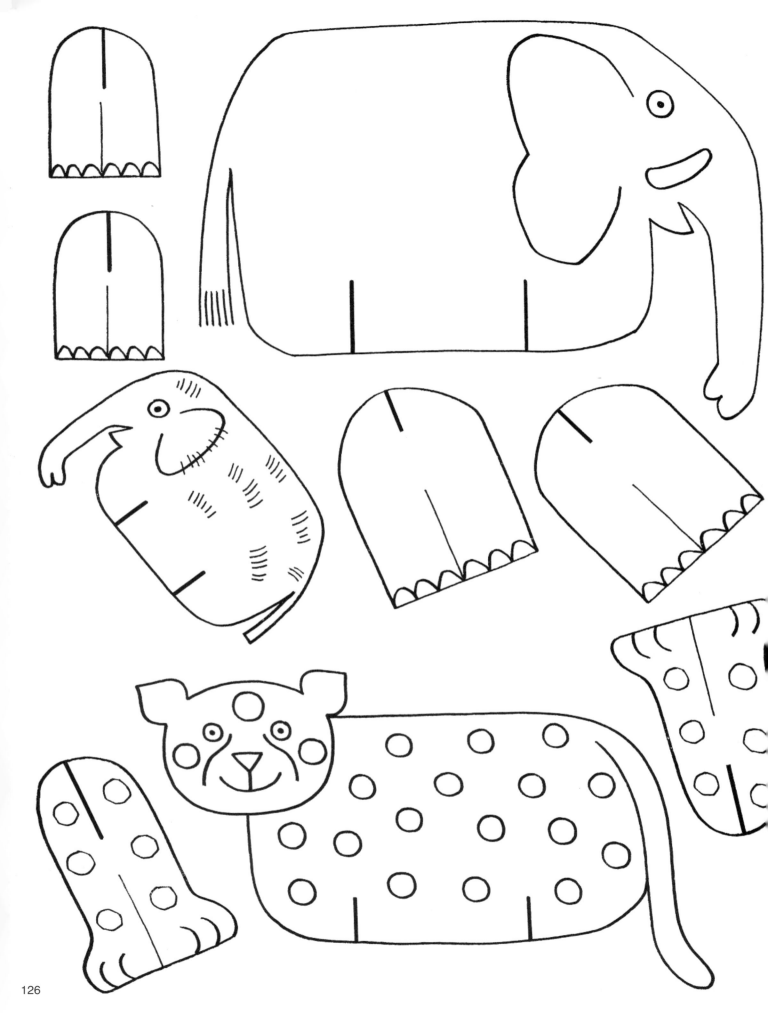

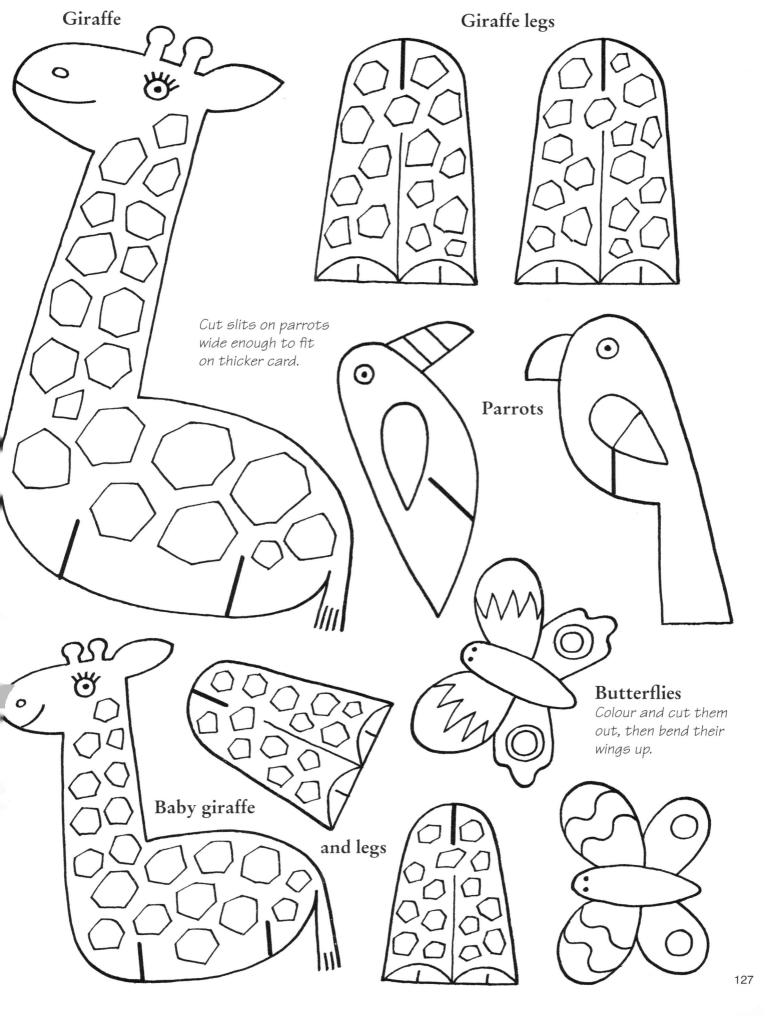

Giraffe

Giraffe legs

Cut slits on parrots
wide enough to fit
on thicker card.

Parrots

Butterflies
Colour and cut them
out, then bend their
wings up.

Baby giraffe

and legs